Fifth Edition

Machine Transcription
and Dictation

Mitsy Ballentine
Greenville Technical College
Greenville, SC

THOMSON
SOUTH-WESTERN

Australia · Canada · Mexico · Singapore · Spain · United Kingdom · United States

THOMSON

SOUTH-WESTERN

Machine Transcription and Dictation, 5th edition

Mitsy Ballentine

VP/Editorial Director:
Jack W. Calhoun

VP/Editor-in-Chief:
Dave Shaut

Senior Publisher:
Karen Schmohe

Acquisitions Editor:
Joseph Vocca

Project Manager:
Dr. Inell Bolls

Production Manager:
Patricia Matthews Boies

Production Editor:
Colleen A. Farmer

Vice President/Director of Marketing:
Carol Volz

Marketing Manager:
Lori Pegg

Marketing Coordinator:
Georgi Wright

Manufacturing Coordinator:
Charlene Taylor

Design Project Manager:
Rik Moore

Compositor:
Argosy

Cover and Internal Designer:
Brenda Grannan

Cover Photo Source:
© PhotoDisc, Inc.

Printer:
Edward Brothers

For more information
contact South-Western,
5191 Natorp Boulevard,
Mason, Ohio, 45040.
Or you can visit our Internet site at:
http://www.swlearning.com

Photo Credits

Pages 4, 270 © Susan Van Etten; page 8 bottom, page 97 middle © PhotoDisc Blue/GettyImages; page 8 middle,
284 © Brand X Pictures/GettyImages; page 8 top, page 96 top, 214 © PhotoDisc Green/GettyImages; page 10
© PhotoDisc/GETTY IMAGES; pages 24, 228 © Index Stock Imagery; pages 38, 52, 66, 80, 112, 126, 140, 168,
200, 256 © RF/CORBIS; page 96 bottom © PhotoDisc Red/GettyImages; page 98 © Brand X Pictures/GETTY
IMAGES; page 154 © Digital Vision/GETTY IMAGES; page 184 (all 3), page 242 © Royalty-Free/Corbis; page 186
© Inc. MedioImages/Index Stock Imagery

Machine Transcription and Dictation, 5e

Legal Studies: Terminology & Transcription 5e is a versatile package that includes a text-workbook and CD-ROM for computerized transcription. This comprehensive list of legal terms, accompanied by transcription content, is core information needed by anyone interested in becoming a legal administrative professional or court reporter.

0-538-43722-7 Text/CD Package
0-538-43723-5 Instructor's Resource CD
0-538-43724-3 Windows Site License CD

Legal Office Projects utilizes a project-based approach to completing legal office activities. Serving as a floating legal assistant for a number of diverse individuals practicing various types of law, the user gets a hands-on approach to legal document preparation, layout, formatting and the transcribing of those documents.

0-538-72123-5 Text/Data Disk Package
0-538-72229-0 Instructor's Manual
0-538-72122-7 Audiocassette

Procedures & Theory for Administrative Professionals 5e is designed to prepare the office professional for a challenging role in today's workplace. Employees must be able to adjust to a diversified workforce with emerging technologies and be prepared to function in an expanding and global marketplace.

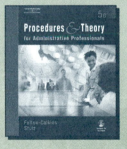

0-538-72740-3 Text/CD Package
0-538-72743-8 Workbook
0-538-72744-6 Instructor's Resource CD

Online Training for the Administrative Professional is a web-based training program that can be used in a distance/distributed learning environment, as a stand-alone unit of instruction, as a supplement to any office course, or for corporate office training. This online program consists of blocks of content covering office skills requested by today's employers and skills that are needed by any office professional.

0-538-72491-9 Complete Set of Modules (12)

Join us on the Internet at www.swlearning.com

THOMSON
SOUTH-WESTERN

Preface

The fifth edition of *Machine Transcription and Dictation* for Document Processing, provides students with the skills needed to transcribe a variety of documents and helps them strengthen their grammar and punctuation skills. This text-workbook provides realistic documents from various fields of employment. Students increase their business vocabulary by learning the spelling and definition of words used in these fields. This edition also includes a section on dictation that gives students the opportunity to actually dictate and transcribe their own work.

This text-workbook is intended for students in vocational schools; adult education programs; career centers; office technology certificate, diploma, and degree programs at the post-secondary level; and secondary students enrolled in office careers courses.

TEXT-WORKBOOK ORGANIZATION

This edition of *Machine Transcription and Dictation* retains all of the popular and educationally sound features of the fourth edition as well as some expanded exercises to reinforce student learning. The text-workbook is structured into four parts with a reference manual at the end of Part 4.

Part 1 covers Basic Machine Transcription, Part 2 Intermediate Machine Transcription, Part 3 Advanced Machine Transcription—Legal and Medical, and Part 4 Dictation and Continuous Speech Recognition. An instructor can assign one or all parts depending on whether this text-workbook is used as a learning unit within a course or as a complete course.

Part 1, Basic Machine Transcription, gives experience in keying documents from various fields of employment. Punctuation is dictated within this part. Part 2, Intermediate Machine Transcription, includes dictation from a variety of international dictators who will give very little punctuation as they dictate. Part 3, Advanced Machine Transcription, concentrates on legal and medical dictation. Students are instructed to review all language skills previously learned because they will be tested on these skills; therefore, learning is reinforced and cumulative. Part 4, Dictation and Continuous Speech Recognition, gives students practice in dictating and transcribing documents. They will learn about the basic concept of continuous speech recognition but will not actually use the technology in this course.

This text-workbook is organized into four parts, with a total of 20 chapters.

KEY FEATURES

- **Getting Started** gives students a job description and step-by-step transcription procedures.

- **Transcription CD** contains dictation files that can be manipulated by foot pedal, mouse clicks, or keystrokes. Templates for all letterheads used with each chapter are also included on the CD.

- **Overview** begins each chapter and includes specific objectives.

- **Proofreading Exercises** are included before each written test to give the students opportunities to correct documents using proofreading marks.

- **Written Tests** are included as well as transcription tests.

- **Word Mastery Previews** include business words that will be in the dictation given for that chapter.

- **Word Mastery Self-Checks** allow students to evaluate their learning of the vocabulary words presented within the chapter. Answers are given at the end of each chapter. Additional exercises have been added to those in the fourth edition.

- **Language Skills** are given to review basic grammar, punctuation, capitalization, and number style.

- **Language Skills Self-Checks** allow students to evaluate their learning of the language skills presented within the chapter. Students may check their answers at the end of each chapter. Additional exercises have been added to those in the fourth edition.

- **Composition Reinforcement Exercise**s are provided to allow students to compose paragraphs utilizing the vocabulary and language skills learned.

- **Collaborative Research** activities promote teamwork and give students the opportunity to use the library and the Internet to seek answers to questions.

- **Transcription Exercises** include directions students need to transcribe the dictation from the CD.

- **Chapter Checkpoints** are included to allow students to assess if they have met the overall objectives of each chapter.

- A **Reference Manual** includes a summary of all language skills presented, examples of formatting, and other helpful resource information.

- **Dictation and Continuous Speech Recognition** is included in this text-workbook that gives students an opportunity to dictate and transcribe material. They will also have the opportunity to learn the basics of continuous speech recognition.

- **Evaluation Forms** for each chapter can be used as a cover sheet for submitting work to the instructor and for the instructor to use to give feedback to the student.

ACKNOWLEDGEMENTS

The author would like to thank all those who contributed support or suggestions for this edition of the text-workbook, particularly Dr. Inell Bolls, project manager at South-Western Business and Professional Publishing; Angela McDonald, consulting editor; and reviewers. The author would especially like to thank family, friends, and students for all of their support. Reviewers who contributed much to this edition are:

Ms. Jennifer Danzer
Vatterott College
Springfield, MO

Ms. Kathy Locke
Spartanburg Technical College
Spartanburg, SC

Ms. Pearl Johnson
Ogeechee Technical Institute
Statesboro, GA

Contents

Getting Started

Electronic technology is constantly advancing. These changes challenge the skills of today's office worker, who needs not only a basic understanding of the business environment but also specific office skills. One of the office skills that remains in demand is machine transcription. While the equipment continues to improve and reflect technological advances, transcription still means the ability to process documents from taped dictation to a computer. Machine Transcription and Dictation *will prepare you for most situations requiring transcription skills.*

MEMORANDUM

TO: Machine Transcription Student

FROM: The Author

DATE: First Day on the Job

SUBJECT: Welcome

This text-workbook has been developed to help you become proficient in transcribing a variety of documents. It is imperative that you read all the introductory information—the Preface, Job Description, and Transcription Procedures—before beginning any of the work in this text-workbook. You will also want to be sure to read and follow all directions in each of the chapters.

Should you have any questions about the information provided, please consult your instructor immediately. The instructor will be your guide as you gain experience and confidence in using the equipment and developing your transcribing skills.

JOB DESCRIPTION

Job Title: Machine Transcriptionist

Job Qualifications:

- Must be able to type 35 wpm and have basic knowledge of Microsoft Word 98 software or higher.
- Must have a basic knowledge of English grammar, punctuation, capitalization, and number style.
- Must be able to read and follow written and verbal directions.

Job Duties:

- Read and complete all activities assigned in a timely manner.
- Transcribe various business documents dictated into acceptable form.
- Proofread and submit all work according to directions.
- Dictate and transcribe material following specified guidelines.
- Keep workstation, computer, and Transcription CD in order.
- Report any problems with computer or the Transcription CD.
- Use reference materials or sources as needed (dictionary, Internet, etc.).
- Work in teams when directed to complete designated assignments.

1. **Prepare Your Workstation**

   Clear your workstation or student desk of everything except the following:
   - A computer with Microsoft Word 98 SE software or higher installed.
   - A printer or access to a printer if you are sharing printers in the classroom.
   - A ⅛" mini-plug headset connected to your computer to use with the Transcription CD.
   - Transcription CD containing Practice Exercise that is part of Chapter 1.
   - Student text-workbook, dictionary, pen or pencil.

2. **Prepare Your Computer**

   Special note regarding use of transcription CD: Depending on the system you are using, you may use a foot pedal, mouse, or keystrokes to start, stop, rewind, and fast-forward your dictation. Your instructor will assist you in determining which method you will use with this course. When you hear the instruction, "Release your foot pedal," you will use your chosen method to stop the dictation.

   The Transcription CD offers you a choice of either Express Scribe (provided free of charge by NCH Swift Sound) or Windows Media Player 9.0 playback software for use while transcribing the dictated files. Instructions for accessing the files for each software application appear below. Recommended minimum system requirements for both software applications are Windows 98SE, ME, 2000 or XP; 233 MHz processor; 64 MB RAM; 100 MB free space on the hard disk; a 3½" floppy drive; and a 16-bit sound card.

   To install the playback application: When the CD is placed into the CD drive, it will automatically start. The student is then offered the choice of installing either Express Scribe (preferred) or Windows Media Player. Click on the button to install the preferred software. The program will be installed on the computer and an icon will be placed on the computer's desktop. Once the software is installed, the student needs to select it from the main menu each time the CD is used.

   Directions for using Express Scribe (foot pedal or keystroke control method):
   a. Plug your headset/foot pedal into the computer using the manufacturer's recommended settings.
   b. Insert the Transcription CD and select "Use Express Scribe" from the main menu.

c. Select the Lesson and the Word Template you wish to open and click the "Launch Lesson" button. The program will automatically open Word and Express Scribe.

d. If you are using hot keys (function keys) to operate the dictation playback, here is a listing of some of the hot keys you will want to use to control the dictation:

F4 Stops the dictation

F9 Plays the dictation

F7 Rewinds the dictation

F8 Fast-forwards the dictation

Important Note to Express Scribe users: The program automatically saves a copy of the audo file in its directory with an 8.3 file name. To avoid confusion, delete these files from Express Scribe's directory upon completion of the lesson.

Directions for using Windows Media Player 9.0 (mouse control method):

a. Plug your headset into the computer using the manufacturer's recommended settings.

b. Insert the Transcription CD and select "Use Windows Media Player" on the main menu.

c. Select the Lesson and the Word template you wish to open, and click on the "Launch Lesson" button.

d. Word will launch, and the Media Player console will appear on top of it. Use your mouse to increase and decrease volume, start and stop, fast-forward to the end or rewind to the beginning. The slider bar may be used to fast-forward and rewind within the dictation lesson.

3. **Complete the Transcription Practice Exercise.**

- Refer to the proper format for reports from the reference manual in the back of this text-workbook.
- Turn to page 6, the Transcription Practice Exercise, and read the directions carefully.
- Insert the CD that contains the Training Practice Exercise into your computer.
- Adjust the volume, speed, and tone on the dictation.
- Key the information you have just heard into your computer.
- Repeat the procedure of listening, stopping the CD if necessary, and transcribing until you have completely keyed the entire practice exercise.
- You may want to stop and replay the dication whenever you need to listen to a group of words again.
- You may also want to fast-forward whenever you need to proceed more quickly through the tape.
- Proofread your document carefully and make all corrections.
- Follow your instructor's directions regarding printing and submitting this practice exercise.

Directions: The diagonals in the first three paragraphs below suggest where you could stop the Transcription CD. Difficult words are spelled out on the CD, and punctuation is dictated so that it will be easy for you to transcribe the report. When you hear the originator (the dictator) say, "Release your foot pedal," always stop the recording and refer to any information given in your text-workbook.

When the dictator wants you to capitalize the first letter of the next word, the dictator will say "Capital." Example: I need to see (Capital) John today. If you are to capitalize the first letter of each major word in the following group of related words, the dictator will say "Caps." Example: I will attend the meeting at the (Caps) American Institute of Technology.

If all letters in each word in the following group of words are to be capitalized, the originator will say "All Caps." Example: Please read the textbook I gave you entitled (All Caps) PROOFREADING MADE EASY.

Listen and transcribe the following dictation for this exercise from the Transcription CD. Use the proper formatting for a report and provide a title for the report that you think would be appropriate. You may refer to the reference manual in the back of this text-workbook for a review of the report format.

The function of/ an office is/ to communicate information./ Information consists of/ words and numbers/ in written or oral form./

The effectiveness/ of an office's operation/ is determined by/ how rapidly and accurately/ office personnel can communicate information/ to other offices internally/ (from office to office within the company)/ and externally (to offices outside the company).

Because of constantly increasing/ amounts of information to process,/ modern offices have been automated/ with electronic machines./ When numbers are processed/ accurately and rapidly/ with calculators and computers,/ it is called "data processing."

Word processing means converting a thought in the originator's mind into written words that are transmitted to a recipient. Words can be processed by writing in longhand or shorthand and by keyboarding.

To increase the speed and accuracy of composing documents, more and more originators are "voice writing" on electronic dictating machines. A transcriptionist then transcribes the documents on an electronic transcribing machine.

Being able to transcribe dictation on a transcribing machine is a valuable asset. There are many jobs now available for machine transcriptionists, and it is predicted that there will be an increasing number of jobs in the future.

Part 1

Basic Machine Transcription

chapter

Machine Transcription

Office professionals who have excellent office skills, good interpersonal skills, superior work ethics, and professional appearance and attitudes are always in great demand. The skills you will learn in this course will be extremely beneficial to you no matter what position or field you may pursue. In addition to operating the equipment and transcribing documents, you will learn how to dictate. You will enhance your language arts and proofreading skills. You will also have the opportunity to transcribe documents used in many different fields of employment.

LEARNING OBJECTIVES

After completing all the learning activities in this chapter, you will be able to:

Define and use the word mastery terms presented in this chapter correctly.

Apply the punctuation and grammar rules for complete sentences, run-on sentences, and fragments.

Apply subject/verb agreement rules presented in this chapter.

Compose paragraphs in acceptable form utilizing the word mastery terms and language skills presented in this chapter.

Utilize your researching, writing, and communication skills correctly in completing a collaborative research activity.

Transcribe documents in acceptable report format.

Directions: In each chapter in this text-workbook, you will be given a list of word mastery terms used in the documents you will be transcribing. Some of the words are unique to the fields in each chapter; some words are simply words that are commonly misspelled.

Learn the definition for each word and how to spell it correctly. Examples of word mastery terms used during the transcription process are given below.

transcribe

Definition: to make a written or typed copy of dictated material
Example: Stephanie's boss asked her to transcribe his speech.

dictation

Definition: words that are dictated by a person or recorded on a tape
Example: When he had taken the dictation from his employer, he immediately began to transcribe the material.

fluency

Definition: ability to flow smoothly
Example: His fluency in using the French language impressed all of us.

rewind

Definition: to turn backwards
Example: You will need to rewind the tape to hear the beginning.

fast-forward

Definition: to move ahead
Example: If you fast-forward the cassette, you can get to the end of the dictation quickly.

valuable

Definition: having considerable worth
Example: Leon considered his knowledge of English skills to be extremely valuable.

machine transcriptionist

Definition: a person who transcribes dictation using a dictation/transcription unit
Example: Robert hoped to obtain a job as a medical machine transcriptionist when he completed his training.

predicted

Definition: foretold or forecasted
Example: The weather station predicted it would rain.

formatting

Definition: putting information into a completed or final form
Example: When she had decided on the proper formatting for the letter, she began to key the document.

reference	*Definition:*	compiled information used as a source
	Example:	What reference material did you use for your report?
rekeying	*Definition:*	to type again
	Example:	Rekeying was necessary because of the numerous errors.
transcription equipment	*Definition:*	equipment used to listen to material that has been recorded
	Example:	Our transcription equipment was broken so we ordered another unit.
centralized	*Definition:*	in one location
	Example:	The filing system was centralized.
microcassettes	*Definition:*	small holders of magnetic tape that are used to record dictation; smaller than minicassettes
	Example:	People use microcassettes to record dictation on the portable units.
minicassettes	*Definition:*	small holders of magnetic tape that are used to record dictation
	Example:	Minicassettes are used with some desktop units.
microphone	*Definition:*	a device used by a speaker to record dictation
	Example:	Please speak directly into the microphone.
originators	*Definition:*	people who create documents
	Example:	You may need to check with the originators to find out if the documents need to be transcribed today.
endless loop	*Definition:*	nonremovable media used to record dictation on a central system. It is a continuous loop; therefore, new dictation records on top of the old dictation.
	Example:	The endless loop on our central dictation system had to be replaced after so many years of use.

WORD MASTERY *Self-Check*

Directions: Complete each sentence by filling in one of the word mastery terms. You may check your answers at the end of this chapter.

1. You will need to listen to the _____ on the tape before you can transcribe the material.

2. If you press the _____ button, you will be able to listen to the information again.

3. The office manager gave the tape to the _____ _____ and asked her to have the material keyed from the tape as soon as possible.

4. When you key the document correctly the first time, you do not have to go through the _____ process.

5. When you are unsure of the correct document _____, you need to review the various styles in a reference manual.

6. Although _____ and _____ have been used to hold recorded dictation in the past, transcriptionists now find most dictation is stored on CDs.

7. A good transcriptionist will keep many _____ books nearby when transcribing to check spelling, format style, etc.

8. Karen and Sarah found having good English and grammar skills was essential when they began to _____ the dictation from their employers.

9. Harry's, Lisa's, and Susan's instructor _____ they would be successful on the job based on their performance in school.

10. Although Orfa had moved from Colombia to America only a year ago, her _____ in English was impressive.

Rule:	A sentence must be a complete thought and contain a subject and a verb. The subject is a noun or pronoun. A noun is a person, place, or thing. A pronoun takes the place of a noun. The word *you* can be an understood subject, which means it is not stated but implied. The verb expresses action or a state of being.
Examples:	• Go to the store. (The subject *you* is implied.) • Mary will give me the information.

Rule:	Do not use two sentences as one sentence. Two sentences must be separated either by a period or a semicolon or a comma with a conjunction.
Examples:	• Rubeanna can handle the job. Joseph will not be able to perform his duties. • Many people would like to own their own businesses; Gabriel has owned his own business for three years. • Keyboarding skills are essential for today's office employee, and the knowledge of various software application packages is certainly desired.

Rule:	A group of words must express a complete thought to be a complete sentence. If the thought is not complete even though it includes a subject and verb, it is a fragment or a dependent clause.
Examples:	• If we have the answers to the problem (Fragment or dependent clause) • If we have the answers to the problem, we can proceed with the experiment. (Complete sentence)

Rule:	Subject and verb must agree in person and number. A singular subject must have a singular verb; a plural subject must have a plural verb.
Examples:	• The document was not received. (*Document* is a singular subject; *was received* is a singular verb expression.) • The documents were received. (*Documents* is a plural subject; *were received* is a plural verb.)

Directions: Make any corrections in the examples below. Then check your answers at the end of this chapter.

1. I will be glad to go to the party.

2. Willis is not going to present the information at the meeting Rachel will be the one to give the presentation.

3. Stop!

4. Because I want to do well in this course.

5. A table, a chair, and a desk is all the pieces of furniture we will need for our office.

6. We need to be sure we are going to have enough material for the presentation we want to be prepared.

7. The cost of the repairs are too high.

8. Let's begin the meeting on time.

9. If we don't understand the reason.

10. The reason for the delays were not explained.

COMPOSITION REINFORCEMENT

Directions: In the spaces provided, compose a paragraph using the word mastery terms, and apply the language skills you have studied. Complete and submit your work for this assignment according to your instructor's directions.

Paragraph 1: Write a paragraph that contains at least two of the word mastery terms used correctly.

_____

_____

_____

_____

_____

_____

_____

Paragraph 2: Explain the term **formatting.**

_____

_____

_____

_____

_____

_____

_____

_____

Paragraph 3: What does it mean to express a complete thought?

_____

_____

_____

_____

_____

_____

Paragraph 4: Write a paragraph that describes the various equipment used for transcription.

_____

_____

_____

_____

_____

_____

Paragraph 5: Describe reference materials that will assist you in your work as a transcriptionist.

_____

_____

_____

_____

_____

_____

COLLABORATIVE RESEARCH

Directions: You have learned some information about machine transcription, and you will transcribe documents in this chapter to help you become accustomed to using the equipment and become familiar with the transcription process. However, in order to learn more about machine transcription, this research activity is provided. You will find this information valuable when you start pursuing employment. This activity will also help increase your researching, writing, and communication skills. In small groups, work together to answer each numbered item.

You may find answers by researching the Internet, newspaper, and library; or you may want to talk with individuals who are actually employed in this field.

When searching the Internet, you may find information about the various fields by searching for the type of field mentioned in the chapter followed by the word *training. Example:* For Chapter 1, use *machine transcription training.*

Complete and submit your work for this assignment according to your instructor's directions.

1. Research the employment opportunities for office workers and list the advantages and/or disadvantages of using machine transcription equipment.

_____

_____

_____

_____

_____

_____

2. List the skills or characteristics that are necessary for someone who wants to do transcription work.

_____

_____

_____

_____

_____

_____

3. List the various job titles or positions in the machine transcription field.

_____

_____

_____

_____

_____

_____

4. List the salary ranges for positions in this field.

_____

_____

_____

_____

_____

_____

_____

_____

5. List any additional information you learned during your research.

_____

_____

_____

_____

_____

_____

_____

Directions: Read the Transmittal Memo, Job Description, and the pages that include the directions for operating your transcribing unit if you have not already done so. Complete the activities included in those pages as well. All of this material is located at the beginning of your text-workbook.

Complete all learning activities in this chapter and read all steps before beginning the transcription exercises.

1. Review the formatting for reports in the reference section at the back of your text-workbook.

2. Use plain paper to print the documents you transcribe in this chapter. In other chapters, you will be using the templates provided on the student's CD.

3. Transcribe the four documents from the student's CD in acceptable report form.

4. Proofread and spell-check each document before submitting all four documents to your instructor according to the instructor's guidelines.

CHAPTER *Checkpoints*

Upon completion of the various learning activities in this chapter, you should be able to meet the objectives listed at the beginning of this chapter. If you feel you cannot answer "yes" to all of the statements listed below, consult your instructor.

Directions: *Place a check mark (✓) in the box for all that apply.*

☐ I can define and use the word mastery terms presented in this chapter.

☐ I can apply the rules presented in this chapter regarding complete sentences, run-on sentences, and fragments.

☐ I can apply the rules presented in this chapter regarding the proper use of subject/verb agreement.

☐ I can compose paragraphs in acceptable form utilizing the word mastery terms and language skills presented in this chapter.

☐ I can use my researching, writing, and communication skills correctly.

☐ I can transcribe reports in acceptable form.

ANSWER KEY FOR *Self-Checks*

Answers to Word Mastery Self-Check

1. You will need to listen to the **dictation** on the tape before you can transcribe the material.

2. If you press the **rewind** button, you will be able to listen to the information again.

3. The office manager gave the tape to the **machine transcriptionist** and asked her to have the material keyed from the tape as soon as possible.

4. When you key the document correctly the first time, you do not have to go through the **rekeying** process.

5. When you are unsure of the correct document **formatting**, you need to review the various styles in a reference manual.

6. Although **microcassettes** and **minicassettes** have been used to hold recorded dictation in the past, transcriptionists now find most dictation is stored on CDs.

7. A good transcriptionist will keep many **reference** books nearby when transcribing to check spelling, format style, etc.

8. Karen and Sarah found having good English and grammar skills was essential when they began to **transcribe** the dictation from their employers.

9. Harry's, Lisa's, and Susan's instructor **predicted** they would be successful on the job based on their performance in school.

10. Although Orfa had moved from Colombia to America only a year ago, her **fluency** in English was impressive.

Answers to Language Skills Self-Check

1. I will be glad to go to the party. (No corrections needed.)

2. Willis is not going to present the information at the meeting. Rachel will be the one to give the presentation. (A semicolon or a comma with a conjunction in place of the period would be correct.)

3. Stop! (No corrections needed. The subject *you* is understood.)

4. Because I want to do well in this course, I will study. (Other words could be added in place of the words *I will study.*)

5. A table, a chair, and a desk are all the pieces of furniture we will need for our office. (Plural subjects take plural verbs.)

6. We need to be sure we are going to have enough material for the presentation. We want to be prepared. (A semicolon or a comma with a conjunction in place of the period would be correct.)

7. The cost of the repairs is too high. (Singular subject takes a singular verb.)

8. Let's begin the meeting on time. (No corrections needed.)

9. If we don't understand the reason, we need to ask for further information. (Other words could be added to complete the sentence.)

10. The reason for the delays was not explained. (Singular subject takes a singular verb.)

Student's Name: _____

Instructor's Name: _____

Class: _____

	Date Work Submitted	Grades (Determined by Instructor)
Composition Reinforcement	_____	_____
Collaborative Research	_____	_____
Transcription Exercises	_____	_____
	_____	_____
	_____	_____
	_____	_____

Instructor's Comments Regarding Work or Suggestions for Improvement:

_____

_____

_____

_____

_____

_____

_____

_____

_____

chapter

Advertising, Journalism, and Publishing

T he fields of advertising, journalism, and publishing are exciting careers especially if you enjoy English and writing. Usually a college education with a major in one of these fields is required for entering into these occupations. Employment in these fields is expected to increase, while keen competition is expected for entry-level jobs.

LEARNING OBJECTIVES

After completing all the learning activities in this chapter, you will be able to:

Define and use the word mastery terms presented in this chapter correctly.

Apply the comma rules presented in this chapter.

Apply the capitalization rules presented in this chapter.

Compose paragraphs in acceptable form utilizing the word mastery terms and language skills presented in this chapter.

Utilize your researching, writing, and communication skills correctly in a collaborative research activity.

Transcribe letters in block style with open punctuation in acceptable form.

Directions: Learn the definition for each word and how to spell it correctly. Examples of word mastery terms used during the transcription process are given below.

proposal

Definition: a plan or an offer to be accepted or rejected

Example: You have submitted a proposal for this project to the correct individual.

autobiography

Definition: an account of a person's life written by her/himself

Example: Shirley MacLaine's autobiography was most unusual.

royalties

Definition: compensation based on a portion of the proceeds

Example: The author did not receive the royalties she had expected.

editor

Definition: a person who has managerial and decision-making responsibilities at a publishing, newspaper, or magazine firm

Example: When the editor approves this text, we can begin printing the material.

accommodate

Definition: to provide or supply

Example: If we can accommodate your needs in any way, please let us know.

commercial

Definition: an announcement advertising or promoting a product

Example: The commercial for our newest product did not draw as much interest as we had hoped.

manuscript

Definition: an author's draft of her/his work

Example: Every manuscript received by our office is reviewed.

fiction

Definition: a piece of work that is not based on true events

Example: Many works of fiction often seem true to life.

expertise	*Definition:*	skill or knowledge
	Example:	Your expertise in English provided the information we needed.
campaign	*Definition:*	a systematic course of action or activities
	Example:	The campaign will start this fall.

Directions: Complete each sentence by filling in one of the word mastery terms. You may check your answers at the end of this chapter.

1. We feel the _____ for the project did not address all the points that need to be covered before we could approve it.

2. Although we can _____ your request for the information, we will not be able to send it to you by the date you desire.

3. Some _____ have been written by individuals, but most people prefer that someone else write about their life than themselves.

4. Our _____ will have to approve all the material before it is released.

5. Because of his _____ in that field, we were able to complete the project on time.

6. The author hoped to receive 10 percent in _____ for his work.

7. When you see a(n) _____ on television, remember its purpose is to entice you to buy the product being advertised.

8. The political _____ was involving more work than anticipated.

9. If you like to read material based on true facts, then you would want to read nonfiction rather than _____ books.

10. The reviewers were impressed with the author's first _____ for his book.

Directions: Review basic grammar and punctuation rules. These rules also appear in the reference manual at the back of your text-workbook.

Rule:	Use a comma to set off a dependent clause at the beginning of a sentence from the independent clause.
Example:	• If the package doesn't come this morning, call me.
Rule:	Use a comma or commas to set off a word or words that rename words they follow.
Example:	• My best friend, Maria Sieradzki, moved away several weeks ago.
Rule:	Use a comma to set off parenthetical words or phrases that are needed in the sentence.
Example:	• George, for example, has already completed his report.
Rule:	Capitalize only the first letter of the important words in headings and titles. Conjunctions, articles, and prepositions are not normally capitalized unless they are the first word of the heading or title. Titles of books should be italicized or underlined or keyed in all capital letters.
Example:	• *Alice in Wonderland* was a success for Lewis Carroll.

Directions: Insert commas where needed and provide the correct capitalization in the examples below. Then check your answers at the end of this chapter.

1. If we receive the information in time we can complete our project.

2. My English teacher Mr. Jackson has taught at our school for over 32 years.

3. We can of course expect to have a large group attend the wedding.

4. I did not enjoy reading the book entitled *up on a mountain*.

5. *Gone with the wind* was a book before it became a movie.

6. Of course we hope to complete your project on time.

7. Jacob Nanney our editor will have to approve the material.

8. When we receive the material, we will be able to process your order.

9. As we review the manuscript we can determine what changes need to be made.

10. If you want to consider a career in journalism you will have to have excellent English skills.

COMPOSITION REINFORCEMENT

Directions: In the spaces provided, compose a paragraph using the word mastery terms, and apply the language skills you have studied. Complete and submit your work for this assignment according to your instructor's directions.

Paragraph 1: Explain the difference between an autobiography and a work of fiction.

_____

_____

_____

_____

_____

_____

_____

_____

Paragraph 2: List in paragraph form some editorial responsibilities and decisions.

_____

_____

_____

_____

_____

_____

_____

_____

_____

Paragraph 3: What skills and knowledge might help you prepare a manuscript for publication?

_____

_____

_____

_____

_____

Paragraph 4: Explain some of the uses of commas.

_____

_____

_____

_____

_____

_____

Paragraph 5: What are some of the important details to remember when capitalizing headings and titles?

_____

_____

_____

_____

_____

_____

COLLABORATIVE RESEARCH

Directions: In small groups, work together to answer each numbered item. You may find answers by researching the Internet, newspaper, and library; or you may want to talk with individuals who are actually employed in these fields.

When searching the Internet, you may want to go to **http://www .bls.gov**, click on Publications and Research Papers, click on Occupational Outlook Handbook, and click on the Index to the Handbook for the letter that begins with the word of the field. *Example:* Click on the letter, A, and scroll down the screen to find information on advertising. You also may find information by searching under the name of the field/industry mentioned in the chapter followed by the words *career* or *training. Example:* advertising *career* or *advertising training.*

Complete and submit your work for this assignment according to your instructor's directions.

1. Research the employment opportunities for office workers and list the advantages and/or disadvantages of employment in the advertising, journalism, or publishing fields.

_____

_____

_____

_____

_____

_____

_____

2. List the skills or characteristics that are necessary to work in these fields.

_____

_____

_____

_____

_____

_____

_____

3. List the various job titles or positions in these fields.

_____

_____

_____

_____

_____

_____

4. List the salary ranges for positions in these fields.

_____

_____

_____

_____

_____

_____

_____

5. List any additional information you learned during your research.

_____

_____

_____

_____

_____

_____

_____

Directions: Complete all learning activities in this chapter and read all steps before beginning the transcription exercises.

1. Review the format for a block letter with open punctuation in the reference manual at the end of your text-workbook.

2. Retrieve the file from the student's CD for each document to be transcribed.
   - For Document 1, open TE2-1, the letterhead for Robertson, Jones & McMillan Publishing Company.
   - For Document 2, open TE2-2, the letterhead for KBCM Radio Station.

   - For Document 3, open TE2-3, the letterhead for Robertson, Jones & McMillan Publishing Company.
   - For Document 4, open TE2-4, the letterhead for King Advertising.

3. When you have transcribed a document using the file from the student's CD, remember to use the Save As feature and the name of the individual to whom the document was addressed as the filename for each document.

4. Transcribe all four documents in acceptable form using the current date.

5. Proofread, spell-check, and submit all four documents to your instructor for approval.

CHAPTER *Checkpoints*

Upon completion of the various learning activities in this chapter, you should be able to meet the objectives listed at the beginning of this chapter. If you feel you cannot answer "yes" to all of the statements listed below, consult your instructor.

Directions: *Place a check mark (✓) in the box for all that apply.*

☐ I can define and use the word mastery terms presented in this chapter.

☐ I can apply the comma rules presented in this chapter.

☐ I can apply the capitalization rules presented in this chapter.

☐ I can compose paragraphs in acceptable form utilizing the word mastery terms and language skills presented in this chapter.

☐ I can use my researching, writing, and communication skills correctly.

☐ I can transcribe block letters with open punctuation in acceptable form.

Answers to Word Mastery Self-Check

1. We feel the **proposal** for the project did not address all the points that need to be covered before we could approve it.
2. Although we can **accommodate** your request for the information, we will not be able to send it to you by the date you desire.
3. Some **autobiographies** have been written by individuals, but most people prefer that someone else write about their life than themselves.
4. Our **editor** will have to approve all the material before it is released.
5. Because of his **expertise** in that field, we were able to complete the project on time.
6. The author hoped to receive 10 percent in **royalties** for his work.
7. When you see a **commercial** on television, remember its purpose is to entice you to buy the product being advertised.
8. The political **campaign** was involving more work than anticipated.
9. If you like to read material based on true facts, then you would want to read nonfiction rather than **fiction** books.
10. The reviewers were impressed with the author's first **manuscript** for his book.

Answers to Language Skills Self-Check

1. If we receive the information in time, we can complete our project.
2. My English teacher, Mr. Jackson, has taught at our school for over 32 years.
3. We can, of course, expect to have a large group attend the wedding.
4. I did not enjoy reading the book entitled *Up on a Mountain.*
5. *Gone with the Wind* was a book before it became a movie.
6. Of course, we hope to complete your project on time.
7. Jacob Nanney, our editor, will have to approve the material.
8. When we receive the material, we will be able to process your order. (No corrections needed.)
9. As we review the manuscript, we can determine what changes need to be made.
10. If you want to consider a career in journalism, you will have to have excellent English skills.

Student's Name: _____

Instructor's Name: _____

Class: _____

	Date Work Submitted	Grades (Determined by Instructor)
Composition Reinforcement	_____	_____
Collaborative Research	_____	_____
Transcription Exercises	_____	_____
	_____	_____
	_____	_____
	_____	_____

Instructor's Comments Regarding Work or Suggestions for Improvement:

_____

_____

_____

_____

_____

_____

_____

_____

_____

3

Education, Government, and Public Service

The fields of education, government, and public service offer challenging careers that are rewarding especially if you enjoy helping or serving others. Usually a bachelor's or master's degree is required for a teaching position. Teachers must be licensed in the state in which they are employed. Licensure programs are also required. Government and public service workers must have a high school diploma, and postsecondary training is also desired; many positions require specialized training. Employment in these fields is expected to grow faster than average.

LEARNING OBJECTIVES

After completing all the learning activities in this chapter, you will be able to:

Define and use the word mastery terms presented in this chapter correctly.

Apply the comma and apostrophe rules presented in this chapter.

Compose paragraphs in acceptable form utilizing the word mastery terms and language skills presented in this chapter.

Utilize your researching, writing, and communication skills correctly in a collaborative research activity.

Transcribe letters in modified block style with mixed punctuation in acceptable form.

Directions: Learn the definition for each word and how to spell it correctly. Examples of word mastery terms used during the transcription process are given below.

principal	*Definition:*	head or director of a school
	Example:	The principal decided to hire three new teachers.
recommendation	*Definition:*	advice
	Example:	My recommendation would be to cancel the class.
credentials	*Definition:*	anything that provides the basis for confidence, belief, or credit
	Example:	He received his teaching credentials from the State Board of Education.
retention	*Definition:*	the act of retaining or keeping
	Example:	Our retention rate of students is very good this year.
probationary	*Definition:*	conditional
	Example:	Your contract is probationary until you have completed six months of teaching.
municipal	*Definition:*	pertaining to the local government—town or city
	Example:	Municipal bonds were sold last month.
constituent	*Definition:*	one who authorizes another to act for him/her as representative; a client
	Example:	The constituents from Montana were not going to vote for their congressman again.
restraints	*Definition:*	the acts of controlling or holding back
	Example:	Restraints had to be made on her demands.
felonies	*Definition:*	any serious crime such as murder or burglary
	Example:	Felonies are committed every day in our state.
misdemeanor	*Definition:*	a transgression or offense less than a felony
	Example:	We cannot overlook even the smallest misdemeanor.

subversive

Definition:	tending to overthrow an establishment
Example:	Subversive behavior will not be tolerated in our nation.

appeal

Definition:	request for a review of a case or issue
Example:	The defendant's attorney made an appeal to the Fifth Circuit Court of Appeals.

judgment

Definition:	the judicial decision of a cause in court
Example:	You can appeal the judgment made in court.

prosecution

Definition:	the instituting and carrying out of legal proceedings against a person
Example:	His prosecution could not be delayed any longer.

ordinance

Definition:	regulation
Example:	There is a municipal ordinance against this type of behavior.

Directions: Complete each sentence by filling in one of the word mastery terms. You may check your answers at the end of this chapter.

1. The committee did not want my _____ regarding the issue.

2. Most companies require a(n) _____ period for all new employees.

3. Her _____ was denied by the Supreme Court.

4. _____ for the crimes he committed was done quickly.

5. Although many _____ may be listed, some are never enforced.

6. Many people commit _____ every day.

7. She was arrested and will serve time for the _____ she committed.

8. If you want to teach school, you have to possess certain _____.

9. The _____ rate of the students in Mrs. Buck's class was excellent.

10. Do you plan to appeal the _____ the court rendered?

Directions: Review basic grammar and punctuation rules. These rules also appear in the reference manual at the back of your text-workbook.

Rule:	Use a comma to set off the name of a city from the name of the state and the name of the state from the rest of the sentence.
Example:	• We often visit Denver, Colorado, during the skiing season.
Rule:	Use a comma to set off a series of three or more words, phrases, or clauses unless each word, phrase, or clause is separated by a conjunction. Be sure to put a comma before the last item in the series.
Examples:	• Jeremy, Doug, David, and Mark were chosen to play first string on the basketball team.
	• Anna and Amy and Amanda are all names that begin with the same letter.
Rule:	Use a comma to set off introductory words or phrases.
Examples:	• Consequently, we had to stop the meeting because the debate was so heated.
	• In the meantime, we will go ahead with our presentation.
Rule:	Use an apostrophe to form the possessive of nouns. For all singular nouns, add an *'s*. For a plural noun not ending in *s*, add *'s*. For a plural noun ending in *s*, add an apostrophe after the *s*.
Examples:	• The secretary's desk was not as large as the boss's desk.
	• All women's purses are on sale this week.
	• Our sales associates' bonuses were larger than usual this year.

Directions: Insert commas and apostrophes where needed in the examples below. Then check your answers at the end of this chapter.

1. Portland Oregon is a beautiful city to visit.

2. Needless to say, we enjoy getting together and singing and dancing.

3. Our dinner included a salad an entrée and a dessert.

4. The Young Girls Department is located on the second floor.

5. He didn't like the mens ties that were on display.

6. We would like to visit Black Mountain, North Carolina because it is so scenic.

7. Incidentally will you be able to vote in the next election?

8. The boys, girls, and infants departments are on the lower level.

9. The womens and mens departments are on the top level of the store.

10. JoAnne, Nancy and Dru passed the teachers' exam the first time.

COMPOSITION REINFORCEMENT

Directions: In the spaces provided, compose a paragraph using the word mastery terms, and apply the language skills you have studied. Complete and submit your work for this assignment according to your instructor's directions.

Paragraph 1: What recommendations would you give to someone wanting to study transcription?

_____

_____

_____

_____

_____

_____

_____

_____

Paragraph 2: Explain how the term **credentials** might be used.

_____

_____

_____

_____

_____

_____

_____

_____

Paragraph 3: Explain how the terms **judgment** and **appeal** relate to one another.

_____

_____

_____

_____

_____

Paragraph 4: Explain the rule regarding commas in a series.

_____

_____

_____

_____

_____

_____

Paragraph 5: Write a paragraph that contains at least two word mastery terms and includes at least one use of a possessive noun used correctly.

_____

_____

_____

_____

_____

_____

COLLABORATIVE RESEARCH

Directions: In small groups, work together to answer each numbered item. You may find answers by researching the Internet, newspaper, and library; or you may want to talk with individuals who are actually employed in thess fields.

When searching the Internet, you may want to go to **http://www.bls.gov**, click on Publications and Research Papers, click on Occupational Outlook Handbook, and click on the Index to the Handbook for the letter that begins with the word of the field. You also may find information by searching under the name of the field/industry mentioned in the chapter followed by the words *career* or *training. Example: educational career* or *educational training.*

Complete and submit your work for this assignment according to your instructor's directions.

1. Research the employment opportunities for office workers and list the advantages and/or disadvantages of employment in the education, government, and public service fields.

_____

_____

_____

_____

_____

_____

_____

_____

2. List the skills or characteristics that are necessary to work in these fields.

_____

_____

_____

_____

_____

_____

_____

_____

3. List the various job titles or positions in these fields.

_____

_____

_____

_____

_____

_____

4. List the salary ranges for positions in these fields.

_____

_____

_____

_____

_____

_____

_____

5. List any additional information you learned during your research.

_____

_____

_____

_____

_____

_____

_____

TRANSCRIPTION EXERCISES

Directions: Complete all learning activities in this chapter and read all steps before beginning the transcription exercises.

1. Review the format for modified block letter with mixed punctuation as well as enclosure notations in the reference manual at the end of your text-workbook.

2. Retrieve the file from the student's CD for each document to be transcribed.
   - For Document 1, open TE3-1, the letterhead for Brookwood Community College.
   - For Document 2, open TE3-2, the letterhead for Mayor Jerome Jordan.
   - For Document 3, open TE3-3, the letterhead for Kingsbury Police Department.
   - For Document 4, open TE3-4, the letterhead for Kingsbury Police Department.

3. When you have transcribed a document using the file from the CD, remember to use the Save As feature and the name of the individual to whom the document was addressed as the filename for each document.

4. Transcribe all four documents in acceptable form using the current date.

5. Proofread, spell-check, and submit all four documents to your instructor for approval.

CHAPTER *Checkpoints*

Upon completion of the various learning activities in this chapter, you should be able to meet the objectives listed at the beginning of this chapter. If you feel you cannot answer "yes" to all of the statements listed below, consult your instructor.

Directions: *Place a check mark (✔) in the box for all that apply.*

☐ I can define and use the word mastery terms presented in this chapter.

☐ I can apply the comma rules presented in this chapter.

☐ I can apply the apostrophe rules presented in this chapter.

☐ I can compose paragraphs in acceptable form utilizing the word mastery terms and language skills presented in this chapter.

☐ I can use my researching, writing, and communication skills correctly.

☐ I can transcribe letters in modified block style with mixed punctuation in acceptable form.

Answers to Word Mastery Self-Check

1. The committee did not want my **recommendation** regarding the issue.
2. Most companies require a **probationary** period for all new employees.
3. Her **appeal** was denied by the Supreme Court.
4. **Prosecution** for the crimes he committed was done quickly.
5. Although many **ordinances** may be listed, some are never enforced.
6. Many people commit **misdemeanors** every day.
7. She was arrested and will serve time for the **felonies** she committed.
8. If you want to teach school, you have to possess certain **credentials**.
9. The **retention** rate of the students in Mrs. Buck's class was excellent.
10. Do you plan to appeal the **judgment** the court rendered?

Answers to Language Skills Self-Check

1. Portland, Oregon, is a beautiful city to visit.
2. Needless to say, we enjoy getting together and singing and dancing. (No corrections needed.)
3. Our dinner included a salad, an entrée, and a dessert.
4. The Young Girls' Department is located on the second floor.
5. He didn't like the men's ties that were on display.
6. We would like to visit Black Mountain, North Carolina, because it is so scenic.
7. Incidentally, will you be able to vote in the next election?
8. The boys', girls', and infants' departments are on the lower level.
9. The women's and men's departments are on the top level of the store.
10. JoAnne, Nancy, and Dru passed the teachers' exam the first time.

Student's Name: _____

Instructor's Name: _____

Class: _____

	Date Work Submitted	Grades (Determined by Instructor)
Composition Reinforcement	_____	_____
Collaborative Research	_____	_____
Transcription Exercises	_____	_____
	_____	_____
	_____	_____
	_____	_____

Instructor's Comments Regarding Work or Suggestions for Improvement:

_____

_____

_____

_____

_____

_____

_____

_____

_____

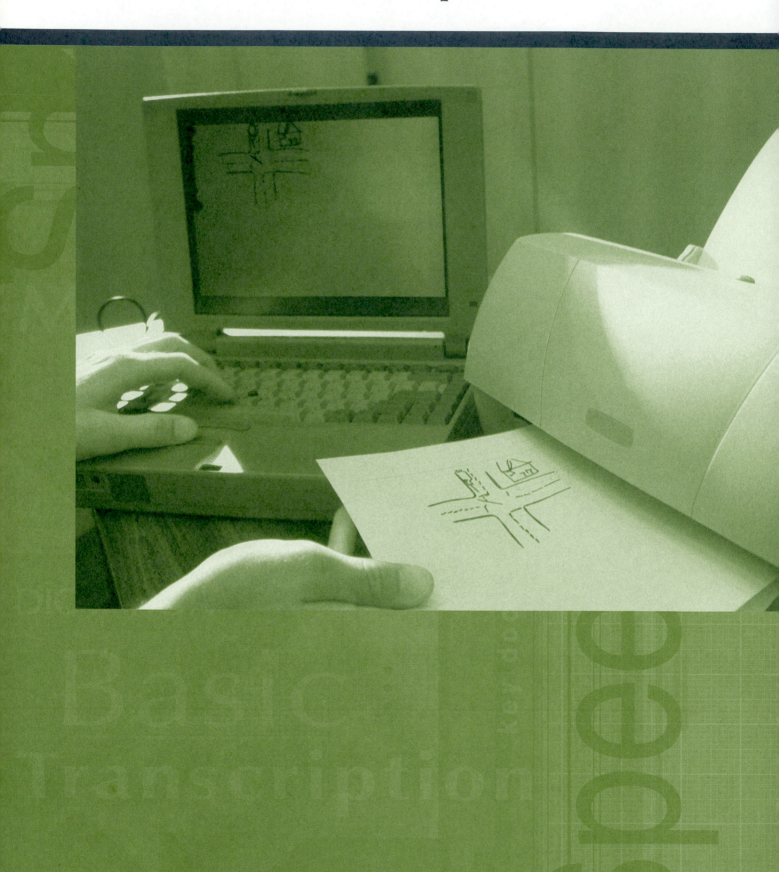

Real Estate, Appraising, and Property Management

The field of real estate, appraising, and property management appeals to those individuals who like to sell or manage various types of property. The two basic types of property are commercial, referring to properties for business and industry, and residential, referring to real estate for private individuals. Most positions require a high school diploma, and postsecondary training is desirable. Specialized training and licensing are required to sell and appraise property. Employment in these fields is expected to grow rapidly in the areas of the country that are experiencing population growth.

LEARNING OBJECTIVES

After completing all the learning activities in this chapter, you will be able to:

Define and use the word mastery terms presented in this chapter correctly.

Apply the comma, hyphen, and semicolon rules presented in this chapter.

Apply the rules for house numbers and street names presented in this chapter.

Compose paragraphs in acceptable form utilizing the word mastery terms and language skills presented in this chapter.

Utilize your researching, writing, and communication skills correctly in a collaborative research activity.

Transcribe letters and memorandums in acceptable form.

Directions: Learn the definition for each word and how to spell it correctly. Examples of word mastery terms used during the transcription process are given below.

| **available** | *Definition:* | suitable or ready |
| | *Example:* | Your new property will be available next month. |

| **opportunity** | *Definition:* | a chance |
| | *Example:* | We hope you will take advantage of this opportunity to increase your knowledge of the subject. |

| **townhouse** | *Definition:* | a group of homes that are joined by common walls |
| | *Example:* | Unfortunately, the fire that occurred in one townhouse caused damage to the other townhouses as well. |

| **ranch home** | *Definition:* | any house with one story |
| | *Example:* | Many older people prefer ranch homes instead of two-story homes. |

| **relocation** | *Definition:* | the process of moving |
| | *Example:* | Relocation from one state to another can be expensive. |

| **client** | *Definition:* | a customer |
| | *Example:* | Be sure to give your client excellent customer service. |

| **commercial property** | *Definition:* | land or buildings for business use |
| | *Example:* | Commercial property is very expensive. |

| **residential property** | *Definition:* | land or buildings for one's own home |
| | *Example:* | With the new subdivision that has been developed, there will be more residential property available. |

| **wheelchair-accessible** | *Definition:* | designed for wheelchair mobility |
| | *Example:* | All businesses must have wheelchair-accessible entrances. |

| **lease** | *Definition:* | rent |
| | *Example:* | I would like to lease the building for my new business. |

| **approximately** | *Definition:* | nearly exact |
| | *Example:* | Unfortunately, the trip was approximately one hour longer than we had expected. |

licensee	*Definition:*	a person to whom a license has been issued or granted
	Example:	The contract was given to the licensee.
brokerage	*Definition:*	the business of a person who sells or buys for a commission
	Example:	The brokerage company will charge a fee for selling your home.
fiduciary	*Definition:*	trustworthy
	Example:	Fiduciary transactions should be the goal of every business.
confidentiality	*Definition:*	the act of keeping something private
	Example:	Confidentiality applies to all business transactions.
disclosure	*Definition:*	the act of revealing
	Example:	The disclosure statement included the structural problems with the building.
diligence	*Definition:*	persistent or constant effort
	Example:	Diligence and time are sometimes required in selling property.
pertinent	*Definition:*	relevant or relating to the matter at hand
	Example:	We must be sure to include all pertinent information in the contract.

Directions: Complete each sentence by filling in one of the word mastery terms. You may check your answers at the end of this chapter.

1. I do not know when my employer will be _____ to take your call.

2. A new _____ will be contacting me about the sale of her home.

3. _____ three new employees will be hired.

4. _____ in this matter must be upheld.

5. If you want to succeed, you will have to use _____ in pursuing your goal.

6. When an excellent _____ comes to buy the home you want, you should take advantage of it.

7. _____ from one branch office to another often occurs in today's business world.

8. Many businesses _____ their office buildings rather than purchase them.

9. All _____ information should be disclosed to the buyers.

10. Not all businesses conduct _____ transactions.

Directions: Review basic grammar and punctuation rules. These rules also appear in the reference manual at the back of your text-workbook.

Rule:	Use a semicolon between clauses in a compound sentence that are not joined by a conjunction.
Example:	• I often enjoy reading a good book; I don't have time to watch television.
Rule:	Use a comma to separate two independent clauses that are joined by the conjunctions *and, but, for, nor, or, yet*. The comma is placed before the conjunction.
Example:	• I left the office very quickly, and I must have forgotten my briefcase.
Rule:	Use a hyphen to join compound adjectives before a noun they modify as a unit.
Example:	• The well-known author died last month.
Rule:	Use a comma to separate two adjectives that are of equal rank and modify the same noun. The word *and* could be placed between these adjectives, and the sentence would still read correctly.
Example:	• The intelligent, beautiful woman was her daughter.
Rule:	Spell out the house number *one* and use figures for all other house numbers. Spell out numbers ten and below used for the names of streets; use figures for numbers above ten used as street names.
Example:	• His new office is located at One Ninth Avenue, and his home is located at 27 East 12th Avenue.

Directions: Insert commas, hyphens, and semicolons as needed, and give the correct usage for numbers in the examples below. Then check your answers at the end of this chapter.

1. Some people prefer to work during the day some people prefer to work at night.

2. I don't know the answer to the question but I am sure Susan could provide the information you need.

3. The middle aged woman did not look a day over thirty.

4. Many people desire an exciting rewarding career.

5. 1 Main Street was his old address 14 5th Avenue will be his new address after the first of the year.

6. Everyone wants to own his or her own home but everyone cannot afford to do so.

7. If you want a well built house, be sure to select a good builder.

8. She used to live on 8th Street.

9. Carmen is an excellent well trained realtor.

10. We moved from 22nd Avenue last year.

COMPOSITION REINFORCEMENT

Directions: In the spaces provided, compose a paragraph using the word mastery terms, and apply the language skills you have studied. Complete and submit your work for this assignment according to your instructor's directions.

Paragraph 1: Give examples of both residential and commercial property. At least one time in your paragraph, use a comma to separate two independent clauses joined by a conjunction.

_____

_____

_____

_____

_____

_____

_____

Paragraph 2: Using word mastery terms correctly, list some pertinent information a buyer (client) might need to know.

_____

_____

_____

_____

_____

_____

_____

_____

Paragraph 3: What is the importance of confidentiality in a business setting?

_____

_____

_____

_____

_____

_____

Paragraph 4: When should actual numerals be used in addresses; when should they be spelled out?

_____

_____

_____

_____

_____

_____

Paragraph 5: Explain the term **opportunity** as it might relate to this class. Properly use a semicolon at least one time in your explanation.

_____

_____

_____

_____

_____

_____

COLLABORATIVE RESEARCH

Directions: In small groups, work together to answer each numbered item. You may find answers by researching the Internet, newspaper, and library; or you may want to talk with individuals who are actually employed in these fields.

When searching the Internet, you may want to go to **http://www .bls.gov**, click on Publications and Research Papers, click on Occupational Outlook Handbook, and click on the Index to the Handbook for the letter that begins with the word of the field. You also may find information by searching under the name of the field/industry mentioned in the chapter followed by the words *career* or *training. Example: real estate career or real estate training.*

Complete and submit your work for this assignment according to your instructor's directions.

1. Research the employment opportunities for office workers and list the advantages and/or disadvantages of employment in the real estate, appraising, and property management fields.

_____

_____

_____

_____

_____

_____

_____

2. List the skills or characteristics that are necessary to work in these fields.

_____

_____

_____

_____

_____

_____

_____

_____

3. List the various job titles or positions in these fields.

_____

_____

_____

_____

_____

_____

4. List the salary ranges for positions in these fields.

_____

_____

_____

_____

_____

_____

_____

5. List any additional information you learned during your research.

_____

_____

_____

_____

_____

_____

_____

Directions: Complete all learning activities in this chapter and read all steps before beginning the transcription exercises.

1. Review the format for block and modified block letters with open and mixed punctuation and memorandums in the reference manual at the end of your text-workbook.

2. Retrieve the file from the student's CD for each document to be transcribed.
   - For Document 1, open TE4-1, the letterhead for Jefferson Real Estate Company.
   - For Document 2, open TE4-2, the letterhead for Jefferson Real Estate Company.

   - For Document 3, open TE4-3, the letterhead for Becker Residential Property Management.
   - For Document 4, open TE4-4, the letterhead for Chicago Commercial Property Management Incorporated.

3. When you have transcribed a document using the file from the student's CD, remember to use the Save As feature and the name of the individual to whom the document was addressed as the filename for each document.

4. Transcribe all four documents in acceptable form using the current date. Use block letter style and mixed punctuation for Document 1. Use the standard memorandum form for Documents 2 and 4. Use a modified block letter style and open punctuation for Document 3.

5. Proofread, spell-check, and submit all four documents to your instructor for approval.

CHAPTER *Checkpoints*

Upon completion of the various learning activities in this chapter, you should be able to meet the objectives listed at the beginning of this chapter. If you feel you cannot answer "yes" to all of the statements listed below, consult your instructor.

Directions: *Place a check mark (✓) in the box for all that apply.*

☐ I can define and use the word mastery terms presented in this chapter.

☐ I can apply the rules regarding the use of numbers presented in this chapter.

☐ I can use my researching, writing, and communication skills correctly.

☐ I can apply the rules for commas, hyphens, and semicolons presented in this chapter.

☐ I can compose paragraphs in acceptable form utilizing the word mastery terms and language skills presented in this chapter.

☐ I can transcribe letters using block and modified block styles and memorandums in acceptable form.

Answers to Word Mastery Self-Check

1. I do not know when my employer will be **available** to take your call.
2. A new **client** will be contacting me about the sale of her home.
3. **Approximately** three new employees will be hired.
4. **Confidentiality** in this matter must be upheld.
5. If you want to succeed, you will have to use **diligence** in pursuing your goal.
6. When an excellent **opportunity** comes to buy the home you want, you should take advantage of it.
7. **Relocation** from one branch office to another often occurs in today's business world.
8. Many businesses **lease** their office buildings rather than purchase them.
9. All **pertinent** information should be disclosed to the buyers.
10. Not all businesses conduct **fiduciary** transactions.

Answers to Language Skills Self-Check

1. Some people prefer to work during the day; some people prefer to work at night.
2. I don't know the answer to the question, but I am sure Susan could provide the information you need.
3. The middle-aged woman did not look a day over thirty.
4. Many people desire an exciting, rewarding career.
5. One Main Street was his old address; 14 Fifth Avenue will be his new address after the first of the year.
6. Everyone wants to own his or her own home, but everyone cannot afford to do so.
7. If you want a well-built house, be sure to select a good builder.
8. She used to live on Eighth Street.
9. Carmen is an excellent, well-trained realtor.
10. We moved from 22nd Avenue last year. (No corrections needed.)

Student's Name: _____

Instructor's Name: _____

Class: _____

	Date Work Submitted	Grades (Determined by Instructor)
Composition Reinforcement	_____	_____
Collaborative Research	_____	_____
Transcription Exercises	_____	_____
	_____	_____
	_____	_____
	_____	_____

Instructor's Comments Regarding Work or Suggestions for Improvement:

_____

_____

_____

_____

_____

_____

_____

_____

chapter

5

Accounting, Auditing, and Financial Planning

The fields of accounting, auditing, and financial planning are careers for those individuals who are detail oriented and enjoy working with numbers. Postsecondary education and certification may be required. A master's degree and knowledge of computer software are desired. Employment in these fields is expected to grow much faster than average, and competition will remain keen for the jobs with the major firms.

LEARNING OBJECTIVES

After completing all the learning activities in this chapter, you will be able to:

Define and use the word mastery terms presented in this chapter correctly.

Apply the comma and semicolon rules presented in this chapter.

Compose paragraphs in acceptable form utilizing the word mastery terms and language skills presented in this chapter.

Utilize your researching, writing, and communication skills correctly in a collaborative research activity.

Transcribe letters using the simplified letter style and block letter style with open punctuation and a financial report in acceptable form.

Directions: Learn the definition for each word and how to spell it correctly. Examples of word mastery terms used during the transcription process are given below.

examination	*Definition:*	the act of investigating or inspecting
	Example:	An examination of her report must be implemented.
financial	*Definition:*	pertaining to money matters
	Example:	Financial reports are required by businesses.
retained	*Definition:*	held in place
	Example:	Her earnings were retained by her agent.
accordance	*Definition:*	agreement
	Example:	We followed his directions in accordance with the list he gave us.
auditing	*Definition:*	the act of verifying financial records
	Example:	The auditing process revealed numerous errors in their accounts.
conformity	*Definition:*	agreement or accordance
	Example:	Many young people find conformity very confining.
taxpayer	*Definition:*	a person who is subject to paying tax
	Example:	Many taxpayers wait until the last minute to submit their tax returns.

recipients	*Definition:*	a person or thing that receives
	Example:	She gave away her money to several recipients.
Internal Revenue Service	*Definition:*	the agency that is responsible for enforcing tax laws and collecting tax payments
	Example:	He was hired to be an auditor for the Internal Revenue Service.

WORD MASTERY *Self-Check*

Directions: Complete each sentence by filling in one of the word mastery terms. You may check your answers at the end of this chapter.

1. Of course, our _____ was completed in detail.

2. His _____ records were not very accurate.

3. We performed our work in _____ with the regulations set before us.

4. The _____ of the award thanked the audience.

5. By April 15 most people mail their tax returns to the _____ _____ _____ .

6. His earnings were _____ per his instructions.

7. When the _____ process began, many in the accounting department were anxious.

8. Most _____ don't enjoy paying taxes.

9. The accounting practices were in _____ with the regulations they were to follow.

10. Most businesses are required to prepare _____ reports to their investors.

Directions: Review basic grammar and punctuation rules. These rules also appear in the reference manual at the back of your text-workbook.

Rule:	Use a comma to set off a prepositional phrase of four or more words at the beginning of a sentence. Do not use a comma to set off a prepositional phrase of less than four words.
Examples:	• In the first meeting, we elected officers.
	• In June we will get married.

Rule:	Use a semicolon before the conjunction joining two independent clauses if either clause contains one or more commas.
Example:	• Lakisha, of course, is an excellent student; and she is well liked by all her classmates.

Rule:	Use a semicolon before a transitional adverb that joins two independent clauses. A comma follows the adverb.
Example:	• She purchased the text-workbook; therefore, she will be able to read the homework assignment.

Rule:	Use a comma to set off the name of a person you are directly addressing.
Examples:	• Dr. Evans, will you be able to attend the conference?
	• Please open the door, Alice.
	• If you will give us the information, Mr. Jones, we can process your application.

Directions: Insert commas and semicolons as needed. Then check your answers at the end of this chapter.

1. In the spring we will plant our garden.

2. In the early chapters you will learn the rules for using commas.

3. Our class will meet Monday Wednesday and Friday but we will not have class on Tuesday and Thursday.

4. Now is the time to pursue your goals therefore start writing down what you hope to achieve this year.

5. We would like to hear your report Joseph on the benefits of exercise.

6. Sarah Katherine please give the accountant the information he requested.

7. Of course, we can get your tax return processed before the deadline and we will charge you our normal fee.

8. On your last year's tax return we did not list your social security number correctly.

9. We received your tax return however you forgot to sign it.

10. I do not like math therefore I would probably not enjoy the accounting profession.

COMPOSITION REINFORCEMENT

Directions: In the spaces provided, compose a paragraph using the word mastery terms, and apply the language skills you have studied. Complete and submit your work for this assignment according to your instructor's directions.

Paragraph 1: Explain the term **auditing** and use at least two other word mastery terms in your explanation correctly.

_____

_____

_____

_____

_____

_____

_____

_____

Paragraph 2: Are you in accordance with the expectations in this class?

_____

_____

_____

_____

_____

_____

_____

_____

Paragraph 3: Explain the term **conformity**.

_____

_____

_____

_____

_____

Paragraph 4: List some of your responsibilities as a taxpayer. Use at least one example of a semicolon before a transitional adverb joining two independent clauses.

_____

_____

_____

_____

_____

Paragraph 5: Explain the rule regarding a prepositional phrase set off by a comma. Use a previously unused word mastery term.

_____

_____

_____

_____

_____

COLLABORATIVE RESEARCH

Directions: In small groups, work together to answer each numbered item. You may find answers by researching the Internet, newspaper, and library; or you may want to talk with individuals who are actually employed in these fields.

When searching the Internet, you may want to go to **http://www .bls.gov,** click on Publications and Research Papers, click on Occupational Outlook Handbook, and click on the Index to the Handbook for the letter that begins with the word of the field. You also may find information by searching under the name of the field/industry mentioned in the chapter followed by the words *career* or *training. Example: accounting career* or *accounting training.*

Complete and submit your work for this assignment according to your instructor's directions.

1. Research the employment opportunities for office workers and list the advantages and/or disadvantages of employment in the accounting, auditing, and financial planning fields.

_____

_____

_____

_____

_____

_____

_____

2. List the skills or characteristics that are necessary to work in these fields.

_____

_____

_____

_____

_____

_____

_____

3. List the various job titles or positions in these fields.

_____

_____

_____

_____

_____

_____

_____

4. List the salary ranges for positions in these fields.

_____

_____

_____

_____

_____

_____

_____

_____

5. List any additional information you learned during your research.

_____

_____

_____

_____

_____

_____

_____

_____

Directions: Complete all learning activities in this chapter and read all steps before beginning the transcription exercises.

1. Review the format for simplified and block letters in the reference manual at the end of your text-workbook.

2. Retrieve the file from the student's CD for each document to be transcribed.
   - For Document 1, open TE5-1, the letterhead for Private Accounts, Inc.
   - For Document 2, open TE5-2, the letterhead for Private Accounts, Inc.

   - For Document 3, open TE5-3, the letterhead for Coburn-Fish Financial Planners, Inc.
   - For Document 4, open TE5-4, the Instructions for Filing form.

3. When you have transcribed a document using the file from the student's CD, remember to use the Save As feature and the name of the individual to whom the document was addressed as the filename for each document.

4. Transcribe all four documents in acceptable form using the current date. Use simplified letter format for Documents 1 and 2. Use the block letter format with open punctuation for Document 3. Fill in the information dictated to you on the Instructions for Filing form for Document 4.

5. Proofread, spell-check, and submit all four documents to your instructor for approval.

CHAPTER *Checkpoints*

Upon completion of the various learning activities in this chapter, you should be able to meet the objectives listed at the beginning of this chapter. If you feel you cannot answer "yes" to all of the statements listed below, consult your instructor.

Directions: *Place a check mark (✓) in the box for all that apply.*

☐ I can define and use the word mastery terms presented in this chapter.

☐ I can apply the comma and semicolon rules presented in this chapter.

☐ I can compose paragraphs in acceptable form utilizing the word mastery terms and language skills presented in this chapter.

☐ I can use my researching, writing, and communication skills correctly.

☐ I can transcribe letters using the simplified and block style with open punctuation and a report in acceptable form.

Answers to Word Mastery Self-Check

1. Of course, our **examination** was completed in detail.
2. His **financial** records were not very accurate.
3. We performed our work in **accordance** with the regulations set before us.
4. The **recipients** of the award thanked the audience.
5. By April 15 most people mail their tax returns to the **Internal Revenue Service**.
6. His earnings were **retained** per his instructions.
7. When the **auditing** process began, many in the accounting department were anxious.
8. Most **taxpayers** don't enjoy paying taxes.
9. The accounting practices were in **conformity** with the regulations they were to follow.
10. Most businesses are required to prepare **financial** reports to their investors.

Answers to Language Skills Self-Check

1. In the spring we will plant our garden. (No corrections needed.)
2. In the early chapters, you will learn the rules for using commas.
3. Our class will meet Monday, Wednesday, and Friday; but we will not have class on Tuesday and Thursday.
4. Now is the time to pursue your goals; therefore, start writing down what you hope to achieve this year.
5. We would like to hear your report, Joseph, on the benefits of exercise.
6. Sarah Katherine, please give the accountant the information he requested.
7. Of course, we can get your tax return processed before the deadline; and we will charge you our normal fee.
8. On your last year's tax return, we did not list your social security number correctly.
9. We received your tax return; however, you forgot to sign it.
10. I do not like math; therefore, I would probably not enjoy the accounting profession.

Student's Name: _____

Instructor's Name: _____

Class: _____

	Date Work Submitted	Grades (Determined by Instructor)
Composition Reinforcement	_____	_____
Collaborative Research	_____	_____
Transcription Exercises	_____	_____
	_____	_____
	_____	_____
	_____	_____

Instructor's Comments Regarding Work or Suggestions for Improvement:

_____

_____

_____

_____

_____

_____

_____

chapter

Basic Transcription

Banking, Financial Management, and Consumer Credit

LEARNING OBJECTIVES

After completing all the learning activities in this chapter, you will be able to:

Define and use the word mastery terms presented in this chapter correctly.

Apply the comma and number rules presented in this chapter.

Compose paragraphs in acceptable form utilizing the word mastery terms and language skills presented in this chapter.

Utilize your researching, writing, and communication skills correctly in a collaborative research activity.

Transcribe letters in modified block and blocked styles with open and mixed punctuation in acceptable form.

The fields of banking, financial management, and consumer credit can be demanding but fulfilling careers especially if you enjoy analytical work. A bachelor's or master's degree is usually required. Employment in these fields is expected to grow at an average rate, and there will be keen competition for these jobs because the number of applicants will exceed the number of openings.

Directions: Learn the definition for each word and how to spell it correctly. Examples of word mastery terms used during the transcription process are given below.

certificate	*Definition:*	a document serving as evidence
	Example:	We have many certificates to prove our claim.
investment	*Definition:*	money that has been put to use in order to return a profit
	Example:	My investments were not very wise ones.
opportunities	*Definition:*	a situation or condition favorable for attainment of a goal
	Example:	Many people have not had the opportunities you have had to earn a degree.
deposits	*Definition:*	money placed in a bank
	Example:	Our bank does accept night deposits.
draft	*Definition:*	to draw out funds
	Example:	We can draft your account each month for your house payment.
CDs	*Definition:*	abbreviation for Certificates of Deposit; financial instruments issued by the bank that earn interest on the money deposited
	Example:	She has purchased several CDs in the past few years.
yielding	*Definition:*	the act of producing
	Example:	His investments were yielding a good return.
IRA	*Definition:*	abbreviation for Individual Retirement Accounts; a method of investing that will not be withdrawn until retirement
	Example:	Both he and his wife had decided to set up IRAs as one way to plan for their future.
payee	*Definition:*	a person to whom money is paid
	Example:	She wrote his name as the payee for her check.
insufficient	*Definition:*	not enough
	Example:	There were insufficient funds on deposit at the bank.

service charge	*Definition:*	a fee charged by a bank for providing a particular service
	Example:	Barbara was not aware that a service charge would be assessed by the bank.
cashier's check	*Definition:*	a check drawn by a bank on its own funds and signed by its cashier
	Example:	Only accept a cashier's check or cash when you sell your car.
overdraft	*Definition:*	a draft in excess of one's balance
	Example:	Overdrafts on your account could result in checks being returned.
money market	*Definition:*	a type of savings account that earns interest and permits a limited number of withdrawals
	Example:	Tenisha opened her first money market account at her local bank.

Directions: Complete each sentence by filling in one of the word mastery terms. You may check your answers at the end of this chapter.

1. Your parents made a wonderful _____ in your future by helping you with your college tuition.

2. How many people have had the _____ you had to travel the world?

3. Bob forgot to draw a line after the name of the _____ on his check.

4. _____ funds were the reason his check was returned.

5. Gloria had made a(n) _____ on her account without realizing what she had done.

6. She decided to have the health club _____ her monthly membership fee from her bank.

7. The investments Simon made were not _____ a good return.

8. We encourage our customers to make _____ to their savings accounts as often as possible.

9. Because he started saving early through a(n) _____, he was able to retire much earlier than he thought.

10. Sam decided he would not take a charge card but only accept cash or a(n) _____ _____ when he sold the antique desk to the buyer.

Directions: Review basic grammar and punctuation rules. These rules also appear in the reference manual at the back of your text-workbook.

Rule: Amounts of money, except in legal documents, are written in figures. Amounts less than one dollar are written in figures with the word *cents* following. In writing even sums of money, omit the decimal and double zeros.

Examples:
- Our check for $49.52 was mailed today.
- The customer was charged 50 cents for the gum.
- He was charged $5 for the binder he purchased.

Rule: Use a comma to separate a date from the year and the year from the rest of the sentence.

Example:
- On August 31, 2012, he will celebrate his twenty-first birthday.

Rule: Use a comma to separate two unrelated numbers that are beside each other in a sentence.

Example:
- In the year 2000, 50 groups were started that supported his cause.

Rule: Percentages are written in figures followed by a % sign in statistical data or the word *percent* in ordinary writing.

Example:
- We need 25 percent of your report next week.

Rule: Use figures for numbers that follow a reference. The abbreviation for number is *No.* and is used in some references. Use words for numbers that precede a reference.

Examples:
- Please read pages 21 to 35 in your text-workbook.
- We ordered three boxes of No. 10 envelopes for the office.
- Each student will need to prepare five pages for the report she or he will present to the class next week.

Directions: Insert commas where needed and make any corrections in the number expressions in the examples below. Then check your answers at the end of this chapter.

1. I couldn't believe I found $20.00 in the hallway.

2. Each of us contributed $.75 toward his meal since it was his birthday.

3. Several years ago on April 12 2002 we took our first cruise to Alaska.

4. On page 32 12 items have been omitted.

5. We usually tip 15% or more if we feel we have received good service.

6. He opened the first account on June 3 2001 when he was only 15 years old.

7. We found 50 cents under the sofa.

8. Of course, we had hoped to deposit $100.00 each month in savings.

9. Was the ten percent discount given to everyone?

10. In column 22, 11 names were omitted by mistake.

COMPOSITION REINFORCEMENT

Directions: In the spaces provided, compose a paragraph using the word mastery terms and applying the language skills you have studied. Complete and submit your work for this assignment according to your instructor's directions.

Paragraph 1: Explain how a wise investment might help you in the future. Correctly use at least two word mastery terms.

_____

_____

_____

_____

_____

_____

_____

_____

Paragraph 2: List in paragraph form some possible investments using word mastery terms that have not been used.

_____

_____

_____

_____

_____

_____

_____

_____

Paragraph 3: Write a paragraph explaining a **service charge**. Use some different amounts of money in the text to show your understanding of the proper rules for expressing monetary amounts.

_____

_____

_____

_____

_____

_____

Paragraph 4: Explain the difference between writing the word **percent** and using the % symbol.

_____

_____

_____

_____

_____

_____

Paragraph 5: Write about a special occasion and the date on which it happened using the appropriate punctuation.

_____

_____

_____

_____

_____

_____

COLLABORATIVE RESEARCH

Directions: In small groups, work together to answer each numbered item. You may find answers by researching the Internet, newspaper, and library; or you may want to talk with individuals who are actually employed in these fields.

When searching the Internet, you may want to go to **http://www .bls.gov**, click on Publications and Research Papers, click on Occupational Outlook Handbook, and click on the Index to the Handbook for the letter that begins with the word of the field. You also may find information by searching under the name of the field/industry mentioned in the chapter followed by the words *career* or *training. Example: banking career* or *banking training.*

Complete and submit your work for this assignment according to your instructor's directions.

1. Research the employment opportunities for office workers and list the advantages and/or disadvantages of employment in the banking, financial management, and consumer credit fields.

_____

_____

_____

_____

_____

_____

_____

_____

2. List the skills or characteristics that are necessary to work in these fields.

_____

_____

_____

_____

_____

_____

_____

3. List the various job titles or positions in these fields.

_____

_____

_____

_____

_____

_____

4. List the salary ranges for positions in these fields.

_____

_____

_____

_____

_____

_____

5. List any additional information you learned during your research.

_____

_____

_____

_____

_____

_____

Directions: Complete all learning activities in this chapter and read all steps before beginning the transcription exercises.

1. Review the format for modified block and block letters with open and mixed punctuation as well as enclosure notations in the reference manual at the end of your text-workbook.

2. Retrieve the file from the student's CD for each document to be transcribed.
   - For Document 1, open TE6-1, the letterhead for San Francisco Bank and Trust.
   - For Document 2, open TE6-2, the letterhead for Citizens and Southern Savings.

   - For Document 3, open TE6-3, the letterhead for Community National Bank.
   - For Document 4, open TE6-4, the letterhead for Bank of St. Louis.

3. When you have transcribed a document using the file from the student's CD, remember to use the Save As feature and the name of the individual to whom the document was addressed as the filename for each document.

4. Transcribe all four documents in acceptable form. Use the current date on all correspondence unless another date is dictated. Use modified block letter style with mixed punctuation for Document 1. Use modified block letter style with open punctuation for Documents 2 and 3. Use block letter style with open punctuation for Document 4.

5. Proofread, spell-check, and submit all four documents to your instructor for approval.

CHAPTER *Checkpoints*

Upon completion of the various learning activities in this chapter, you should be able to meet the objectives listed at the beginning of this chapter. If you feel you cannot answer "yes" to all of the statements listed below, consult your instructor.

Directions: *Place a check mark (✓) in the box for all that apply.*

☐ I can define and use the word mastery terms presented in this chapter.

☐ I can apply the comma and number rules presented in this chapter.

☐ I can compose paragraphs in acceptable form utilizing the word mastery terms and language skills presented in this chapter.

☐ I can use my researching, writing, and communication skills correctly.

☐ I can transcribe letters using the modified block and block style letters with open and mixed punctuation and enclosure notations in acceptable form.

Answers to Word Mastery Self-Check

1. Your parents made a wonderful **investment** in your future by helping you with your college tuition.
2. How many people have had the **opportunities** you had to travel the world?
3. Bob forgot to draw a line after the name of the **payee** on his check.
4. **Insufficient** funds were the reason his check was returned.
5. Gloria had made an **overdraft** on her account without realizing what she had done.
6. She decided to have the health club **draft** her monthly membership fee from her bank.
7. The investments Simon made were not **yielding** a good return.
8. We encourage our customers to make **deposits** to their savings accounts as often as possible.
9. Because he started saving early through an **IRA**, he was able to retire much earlier than he thought.
10. Sam decided he would not take a charge card but only accept cash or a **cashier's check** when he sold the antique desk to the buyer.

Answers to Language Skills Self-Check

1. I couldn't believe I found $20 in the hallway.
2. Each of us contributed 75 cents toward his meal since it was his birthday.
3. Several years ago on April 12, 2002, we took our first cruise to Alaska.
4. On page 32, 12 items have been omitted.
5. We usually tip 15 percent or more if we feel we have received good service.
6. He opened the first account on June 3, 2001, when he was only 15 years old.
7. We found 50 cents under the sofa. (No corrections needed.)
8. Of course, we had hoped to deposit $100 each month in savings.
9. Was the 10 percent discount given to everyone?
10. In column 22, 11 names were omitted by mistake. (No corrections needed.)

After you have completed Chapter 6, you should complete the proofreading assignment on the following page to help prepare yourself for the tests for Part 1. Follow your instructor's guidelines for completing this assignment. Take the written test and transcription test for Part 1 before proceeding to Chapter 7.

PROOFREADING ASSIGNMENT

THE IMPORTANCE OF PROPRE PUNCTUATION AND SPELING

In these few chapters you have learned several rules pertaining to the propre use of puncuation. Of course, you should never take the subject of puncuation to lightly. I could site several examples of people who have done this and they wish they had not done so. You need to know rules regarding the propre use of commas semicolons and apostrophes. If you have studied carefully you have all ready recieved a strong review of of some of these rules. In the chapters to come you will learn even more rules about puncuation.

Spelling words corectly is also important. Be sure you have studied the list of words that are frequently mispelled and misused. Effect and affect are too words that quiet often confuse students.

Student's Name: _____

Instructor's Name: _____

Class: _____

	Date Work Submitted	Grades (Determined by Instructor)
Composition Reinforcement	_____	_____
Collaborative Research	_____	_____
Transcription Exercises	_____	_____
	_____	_____
	_____	_____
	_____	_____
Proofreading Assignment	_____	_____

Instructor's Comments Regarding Work or Suggestions for Improvement:

_____

_____

_____

_____

_____

_____

_____

Part 2

(signature)

Intermediate Machine Transcription

Insurance

The insurance field includes many types of insurance such as life, health, dental, cancer, automobile, and homeowners. There are also many different positions within the insurance field. They include insurance agents, underwriters, adjusters, and investigators. A high school education is sufficient to qualify for some positions, but a bachelor's degree is preferred. Many positions also require special certification or licensing. Employment projections vary by position within the insurance field.

LEARNING OBJECTIVES

After completing all the learning activities in this chapter, you will be able to:

Define and use the word mastery terms presented in this chapter correctly.

Apply the number, dash, question mark, and quotation mark rules presented in this chapter.

Compose paragraphs in acceptable form utilizing the word mastery terms and language skills presented in this chapter.

Utilize your researching, writing, and communication skills correctly in a collaborative research activity.

Transcribe two letters into block format with open punctuation, one letter into modified block format with open punctuation, and one memorandum in acceptable form.

Directions: Learn the definition for each word and how to spell it correctly. Examples of word mastery terms used during the transcription process are given below.

life insurance	*Definition:*	insurance that provides payments on the death of the policyholder
	Example:	J. D. purchased life insurance from an insurance company.
long term care insurance	*Definition:*	insurance that provides care for those who require custodial care
	Example:	Most people do not realize the value of long term care insurance.
long term disability insurance	*Definition:*	insurance that protects a portion of your income if you become disabled while on the job
	Example:	Because Anne had long term disability insurance, she still received income while she was recovering from her injury.
exclusions	*Definition:*	items not covered under the insurance policy
	Example:	There were numerous exclusions listed in the policy that Jonathan did not read.
limitations	*Definition:*	maximum amounts covered under an insurance policy
	Example:	The limitations were listed on page 15 of the insurance policy.
policies	*Definition:*	insurance documents
	Example:	One should keep insurance policies in a safe deposit box.
dependents	*Definition:*	the individual's spouse or young children who qualify
	Example:	Ruth and Don's dependents were their two daughters.
eligible	*Definition:*	legally qualified to be covered under an insurance plan
	Example:	All employees must work six months with the company before they will be eligible for insurance.
coverage	*Definition:*	protection provided by a policy against risk
	Example:	Do you think you have enough coverage on your home?

COBRA	*Definition:*	abbreviation for Consolidated Omnibus Budget Reconciliation Act; continued insurance coverage that may be obtained if a person loses his or her current health insurance from the employer
	Example:	Because he lost his job, he was eligible for COBRA coverage.
reimbursement	*Definition:*	the act of repayment for medical expenses
	Example:	Stephen hopes to receive his reimbursement quickly.
deductible	*Definition:*	the amount of covered medical expenses you must pay annually before the insurance company pays any benefits
	Example:	Harold exceeded his $200 deductible during his first month of coverage.
out-of-pocket	*Definition:*	the annual maximum amount you must pay before the insurance company will pay benefits
	Example:	Most policies list $1,500 as the out-of-pocket maximum amount per individual.
lifetime maximum benefit	*Definition:*	the maximum amount the insurance company will pay for each person in his or her lifetime
	Example:	Unfortunately, Robert exceeded his lifetime maximum benefit because of major illnesses during his life.

Directions: Complete each sentence by filling in one of the word mastery terms. You may check your answers at the end of this chapter.

1. Mr. Jordan could not find his _____ _____ policy.

2. Because she had three children, she listed all three as her _____.

3. Since she had lost her job and was no longer covered under her company's insurance, she decided to obtain insurance under _____.

4. Shakeeta had met her _____; therefore, her insurance company would pay the rest of her doctor's bill.

5. Many people think they will never use enough insurance to reach their _____ _____ _____.

6. Lisa was not aware that she may need _____ _____ _____ _____ in order to provide for her care when she is older.

7. Many companies offer their employees _____ _____ _____ _____ that will provide a portion of their income should they become disabled while working.

8. One should keep important papers such as one's life insurance _____ in a convenient, secure location.

9. Before an insurance company will pay benefits, an individual will have to pay some _____ expenses.

10. If there are any _____ in an insurance policy, they will be so indicated in the policy.

Directions: Review basic grammar and punctuation rules. These rules also appear in the reference manual at the back of your text-workbook.

Rule:	Spell out numbers up to and including ten; use figures for numbers over ten.
Examples:	• There were four birds sitting on the branch of the tree.
	• Although all the class could not go out to eat together, 13 of the students ate lunch in the canteen.

Rule:	Spell out time used with o'clock. Use figures for time with the abbreviations a.m. and p.m.
Examples:	• We will not have our meeting until two o'clock.
	• Your flight is at 8:15 a.m.

Rule:	Use the dash before a word that summarizes the preceding part of the sentence.
Example:	• Peaches, bananas, and apples—these are my favorite fruits.

Rule:	Use a question mark after a direct question. Do not use a question mark after indirect questions or polite requests.
Examples:	• Would you like to go to the movies tonight?
	• She asked if she could attend the meeting today.
	• May I see you in my office immediately after class.

Rule:	Use quotation marks to enclose direct quotations. Place the period or comma inside the closing quotation marks. The first word of a direct quote always begins with a capital letter.
Examples:	• Heather said, "Our family will not be attending the wedding."
	• "We cannot afford to buy a larger home," her husband stated.

Directions: Make any corrections in the examples below. Then check your answers at the end of this chapter.

1. Which of the ten items did you not receive?

2. We will not be late for the 4 o'clock funeral.

3. Toys, games, and clothes these are the items that many children receive for their birthdays.

4. May we have your answer as soon as possible.

5. Charlene said, "My office needs to be repainted soon".

6. We expected twelve people to attend the insurance meeting.

7. Don't begin the meeting until nine a.m. or you won't have many present.

8. Life, health, automobile, home, disability these are the different types of insurance he sells.

9. Doris said, my sister's insurance will probably be cancelled if she doesn't pay her premiums.

10. Fred said, "that he hoped he could locate his insurance policy in his safety deposit box at the bank."

COMPOSITION REINFORCEMENT

Directions: In the spaces provided, write five paragraphs using the word mastery terms and applying the language skills you have studied. Complete and submit your work for this assignment according to your instructor's directions.

Paragraph 1: Write a paragraph about some items a homeowner's insurance policy might exclude such as trampolines.

_____

_____

_____

_____

_____

_____

_____

_____

Paragraph 2: Write a paragraph about medical expense reimbursement. Include an example of the use of a number between one and ten *and* an example of a number over ten.

_____

_____

_____

_____

_____

_____

_____

_____

Paragraph 3: Write a paragraph inviting people to an insurance information meeting. Use the proper form for numbers and times.

_____

_____

_____

_____

_____

_____

Paragraph 4: Write a list of questions you might want to ask about an insurance policy.

_____

_____

_____

_____

_____

_____

_____

Paragraph 5: Write a short conversation between a new employee and a personnel officer regarding the company insurance policy. Use quotation marks correctly.

_____

_____

_____

_____

_____

_____

_____

COLLABORATIVE RESEARCH

Directions: In small groups, work together to answer each numbered item. You may find answers by researching the Internet, newspaper, and library; or you may want to talk with individuals who are actually employed in this field.

When searching the Internet, you may want to go to **http://www .bls.gov,** click on Publications and Research Papers, click on Occupational Outlook Handbook, and click on the Index to the Handbook for the letter that begins with the word of the field. You also may find information by searching under the name of the field/industry mentioned in the chapter followed by the words *career* or *training*. *Example: insurance career* or *insurance training.*

Complete and submit your work for this assignment according to your instructor's directions.

1. Research the employment opportunities for office workers and list the advantages and/or disadvantages of employment in the insurance field.

_____

_____

_____

_____

_____

_____

_____

2. List the skills or characteristics that are necessary to work in this field.

_____

_____

_____

_____

_____

_____

_____

_____

3. List the various job titles or positions in this field.

_____

_____

_____

_____

_____

_____

4. List the salary ranges for positions in this field.

_____

_____

_____

_____

_____

_____

_____

5. List any additional information you learned during your research.

_____

_____

_____

_____

_____

_____

_____

TRANSCRIPTION EXERCISES

Directions: Complete all learning activities in this chapter and read all steps before beginning the transcription exercises. In Chapters 7–12, very little punctuation will be dictated on the CD. You will be responsible for supplying the correct punctuation. Therefore, you may want to review the punctuation rules studied in the previous chapters. Some of the dictators on the student's CD in these chapters will have distinct accents; listen carefully as you transcribe the dictation.

1. Review the format for block and modified block letters with open punctuation, enclosure notations, and memorandums in the reference manual.

2. Retrieve the file from the student's CD for each document to be transcribed.
   - For Document 1, open TE7-1, the letterhead for Oklahoma State Insurance Company.
   - For Document 2, open TE7-2, the letterhead for Hinson Insurance Agency.
   - For Document 3, open TE7-3, the letterhead for Homeowner's Insurance Company of America.
   - For Document 4, open TE7-4, the letterhead for Insurance of New York.

3. Remember to use the Save As feature and the name of the individual to whom the document was addressed as the filename.

4. Transcribe the four documents from the student's CD in acceptable form using the current date on all correspondence. Use the proper format for a block style letter with open punctuation for Documents 1 and 3. Use modified blocked letter format with open punctuation for Document 2 and memorandum format for Document 4.

5. Proofread, spell-check, and submit all four documents to your instructor for approval.

CHAPTER *Checkpoints*

Upon completion of the various learning activities in this chapter, you should be able to meet the objectives listed at the beginning of this chapter. If you feel you cannot answer "yes" to all of the statements listed below, consult your instructor.

Directions: *Place a check mark (✔) in the box for all that apply.*

☐ I can define and use the word mastery terms presented in this chapter.

☐ I can apply the number, dash, question mark, and quotation rules presented in this chapter.

☐ I can compose paragraphs in acceptable form utilizing the word mastery terms and language skills presented in this chapter.

☐ I can use my researching, writing, and communication skills correctly.

☐ I can transcribe letters using the modified block and block style letters with open punctuation and enclosure notations and memorandums in acceptable form.

Answers to Word Mastery Self-Check

1. Mr. Jordan could not find his **life insurance** policy.
2. Because she had three children, she listed all three as her **dependents**.
3. Since she had lost her job and was no longer covered under her company's insurance, she decided to obtain insurance under **COBRA**.
4. Shakeeta had met her **deductible**; therefore, her insurance company would pay the rest of her doctor's bill.
5. Many people think they will never use enough insurance to reach their **lifetime maximum benefit**.
6. Lisa was not aware that she may need **long term care insurance** in order to provide for her care when she is older.
7. Many companies offer their employees **long term disability insurance** that will provide a portion of their income should they become disabled while working.
8. One should keep important papers such as one's life insurance **policies** in a convenient, secure location.
9. Before an insurance company will pay benefits, an individual will have to pay some **out-of-pocket** expenses.
10. If there are any **limitations** in an insurance policy, they will be so indicated in the policy.

Answers to Language Skills Self-Check

1. Which of the ten items did you not receive? (No corrections needed.)
2. We will not be late for the four o'clock funeral.
3. Toys, games, and clothes—these are the items that many children receive for their birthdays.
4. May we have your answer as soon as possible. (No corrections needed.)
5. Charlene said, "My office needs to be repainted soon."
6. We expected 12 people to attend the insurance meeting.
7. Don't begin the meeting until 9 a.m. or you won't have many present.
8. Life, health, automobile, home, disability—these are the different types of insurance he sells.
9. Doris said, "My sister's insurance will probably be cancelled if she doesn't pay her premiums."
10. Fred said that he hoped he could locate his insurance policy in his safety deposit box at the bank.

Student's Name: _____

Instructor's Name: _____

Class: _____

	Date Work Submitted	Grades (Determined by Instructor)
Composition Reinforcement	_____	_____
Collaborative Research	_____	_____
Transcription Exercises	_____	_____
	_____	_____
	_____	_____
	_____	_____

Instructor's Comments Regarding Work or Suggestions for Improvement:

_____

_____

_____

_____

_____

_____

_____

_____

Engineering, Industrial, and Manufacturing

Branches in the engineering field include electrical, mechanical, civil, industrial, chemical, and architectural engineering. To be an engineer, you need a college degree.

There are several different types of industrial and manufacturing plants that produce a finished product from raw materials. For example, a manufacturing plant might produce men's shirts from cotton.

A college degree is required for executive positions in all of these fields. Many companies also prefer a graduate degree in either field and/or an MBA (master's degree in business administration). These fields require you to have a strong knowledge of computer training. If you have an analytical mind and enjoy seeing a project through to completion, these fields would be of interest to you. Employment opportunities vary depending on the geographical location.

LEARNING OBJECTIVES

After completing all the learning activities in this chapter, you will be able to:

Define and use the word mastery terms presented in this chapter correctly.

Apply the comma, semicolon, colon, dash, and exclamation point rules presented in this chapter.

Compose paragraphs in acceptable form utilizing the word mastery terms and language skills presented in this chapter.

Utilize your researching, writing, and communication skills correctly in a collaborative research activity.

Transcribe four interoffice memorandums in acceptable format.

Directions: Learn the definition for each word and how to spell it correctly. Examples of word mastery terms used during the transcription process are given below.

generators	*Definition:*	electrical device used to convert mechanical energy to electrical energy
	Example:	An alternator on a car is a form of a generator.
reactor	*Definition:*	a device whose primary purpose is to introduce reactance into a circuit
	Example:	Reactors are very large coils used in power plants.
capacitor	*Definition:*	a device for accumulating and holding a charge of electricity
	Example:	The capacitor in your television needs to be replaced.
resistor	*Definition:*	a device used to introduce resistance into an electric circuit
	Example:	They added a resistor to the stereo speaker to balance the current.
transformer	*Definition:*	an electrical device, which by electromagnetic induction, transfers electrical energy from one or more circuits to another set
	Example:	The transformer for the electricity to their home was struck by lightning.
trip	*Definition:*	to open a circuit
	Example:	When he put a paper clip into the wall receptacle, it tripped the breaker.
voltage	*Definition:*	electromotive force or potential difference expressed in volts
	Example:	High-voltage warning signs were placed on the electric wiring.
fiber optics	*Definition:*	a technique of electronic communication through laser light waves; uses flexible threadlike fiberglass or plastic instead of traditional copper wires
	Example:	Fiber optics are used extensively in telecommunications.

robotics	*Definition:*	technology dealing with the design, construction, and operation of robots in automation
	Example:	The use of robotics has increased our production.
CAD/CAM	*Definition:*	the abbreviation for Computer Aided Design/Computer Aided Manufacturing; computer technology used in designing and manufacturing
	Example:	Jake plans to enroll in the CAD/CAM program at his college next spring.
raw materials	*Definition:*	unprocessed goods
	Example:	Raw materials were gathered from various sources to make the completed product.
backlog	*Definition:*	an accumulation of stock or work
	Example:	Because of the backlog, many people will have to work overtime to complete the work.
batches	*Definition:*	a quantity of material or number of things of the same kind made or handled at one time or considered as one group
	Example:	The checks were processed in batches in the operation center of the bank.

Directions: Complete each sentence by filling in one of the word mastery terms. You may check your answers at the end of this chapter.

1. The _____ of the electricity was clearly indicated.

2. Through her training in _____, she was able to use the computer to assist her with her design.

3. If we want to go home by 5 p.m. and not work overtime, we will need to complete all the _____.

4. Ramon prepared several _____ of cookies for the party.

5. The company had too many _____ _____ that needed to be processed into the final product.

6. Since the company has installed _____, they have increased their production.

7. Because the lightning had damaged the _____ that was connected to the store, there was no electricity for days.

8. The _____ at the plant were down, which means all production was halted due to no electrical energy.

9. Power plants have _____ that are large coils used to introduce reactance into a circuit.

10. Don't _____ the breaker by putting anything into the wall receptacle.

Directions: Review basic grammar and punctuation rules. These rules also appear in the reference manual at the back of your text-workbook.

Rule: Use a colon to introduce a listing that is not immediately preceded by a preposition or a verb. *The following, as follows, such as these*, and *thus* are words that usually begin a listing.

Examples:
- I need to see the following people: Jackson Brooks, Meredith Henderson, and Tammy Green.
- Gloria likes to eat hamburgers, pizza, and hot dogs.
- The blouse comes in beige, white, or black.

Rule: Use a dash instead of a comma when emphasizing a repeated thought or statement.

Example:
- You will need to study—study daily—if you want to be successful in this course.

Rule: Use an exclamation point at the end of a thought expressing strong emotion or a command.

Examples:
- Wow! I won a million dollars!
- Don't make me tell you again to clean up your room!

Rule: Use a semicolon between elements in a listing when commas are needed within the elements.

Example:
- Jose has visited Washington, D.C.; Honolulu, Hawaii; and Juneau, Alaska.

Directions: Make any corrections in the examples below. Then check your answers at the end of this chapter.

1. If you plan to graduate by May, you will need to take the following courses this semester Document Production OST 210 Machine Transcription OST 121 and Introduction to Computers CPT 101.

2. We often pick up a quick lunch at McDonald's, Taco Bell, or Burger King.

3. Gee whiz I thought I lost my car keys.

4. We often quite often think of our needs rather than the needs of others.

5. Our company will be represented at the meeting by Leslie Couric director Matt Dillon marketing manager and Daniel Scott supervisor.

6. You must correct that situation immediately and I mean immediately before we have a voltage problem.

7. If you prepare really prepare for your presentation for the robotics convention, you will be more confident.

8. The following topics will be offered at the seminar CAD/CAM, robotics, and fiber optics.

9. He has been transferred three times from the following locations Greenville South Carolina Charleston West Virginia and Charlotte North Carolina.

10. We will post high-voltage signs on the front back and side of the building.

COMPOSITION REINFORCEMENT

Directions: In the spaces provided, write five paragraphs using the word mastery terms and applying the language skills you have studied. Complete and submit your work for this assignment according to your instructor's directions.

Paragraph 1: Make a list of examples of areas in which people use robotics. Use proper punctuation.

_____

_____

_____

_____

_____

_____

_____

Paragraph 2: Relate a story about backlog in an office environment. Use an exclamation point within the body of the paragraph.

_____

_____

_____

_____

_____

_____

_____

_____

Paragraph 3: Write about your favorite parts of this course. Be sure to use a dash within the body of the paragraph to show emphasis.

_____

_____

_____

_____

_____

_____

Paragraph 4: Show that you understand the proper use of a semicolon by writing about classes you have taken or are taking.

_____

_____

_____

_____

_____

_____

Paragraph 5: Show that you understand the proper use of commas by writing about some favorite computer software.

_____

_____

_____

_____

_____

_____

COLLABORATIVE RESEARCH

Directions: In small groups, work together to answer each numbered item. You may find answers by researching the Internet, newspaper, and library; or you may want to talk with individuals who are actually employed in these fields.

When searching the Internet, you may want to go to **http://www .bls.gov**, click on Publications and Research Papers, click on Occupational Outlook Handbook, and click on the Index to the Handbook for the letter that begins with the word of the field. You also may find information by searching under the name of the field/industry mentioned in the chapter followed by the words *career* or *training*. *Example: engineering career or engineering training.*

Complete and submit your work for this assignment according to your instructor's directions.

1. Research the employment opportunities for office workers and list the advantages and/or disadvantages of employment in the engineering, industrial, and manufacturing fields.

_____

_____

_____

_____

_____

_____

_____

2. List the skills or characteristics that are necessary to work in these fields.

_____

_____

_____

_____

_____

_____

_____

_____

3. List the various job titles or positions in these fields.

_____

_____

_____

_____

_____

_____

4. List the salary ranges for positions in these fields.

_____

_____

_____

_____

_____

_____

_____

5. List any additional information you learned during your research.

_____

_____

_____

_____

_____

_____

_____

Directions: Complete all learning activities in this chapter and read all steps before beginning the transcription exercises. In Chapters 7–12, very little punctuation will be dictated on the student's CD. Remember to supply the correct punctuation.

1. Review the format for interoffice memorandums in the reference manual.

2. Retrieve the file from the student's CD for each document to be transcribed.
   - For Document 1, open TE8-1, the letterhead for Acme Electrical Engineering.
   - For Document 2, open TE8-2, the letterhead for Jackson Engineering, Inc.
   - For Document 3, open TE8-3, the letterhead for Southwestern Manufacturing.
   - For Document 4, open TE8-4, the letterhead for Minnesota Manufacturing.

3. Remember to use the Save As feature and use the name of the individual to whom the document was addressed as the filename for each document.

4. Transcribe the four documents from the student's CD in acceptable form using the current date on all correspondence. Use the proper format for interoffice memorandums for all four documents.

5. Proofread, spell-check, and submit all four documents to your instructor for approval.

CHAPTER *Checkpoints*

Upon completion of the various learning activities in this chapter, you should be able to meet the objectives listed at the beginning of this chapter. If you feel you cannot answer "yes" to all of the statements listed below, consult your instructor.

Directions: *Place a check mark (✓) in the box for all that apply.*

☐ I can define and use the word mastery terms presented in this chapter.

☐ I can apply the comma, semicolon, colon, dash, and exclamation point rules presented in this chapter.

☐ I can compose paragraphs in acceptable form utilizing the word mastery terms and language skills presented in this chapter.

☐ I can use my researching, writing, and communication skills correctly.

☐ I can transcribe memorandums in acceptable form.

Answers to Word Mastery Self-Check

1. The **voltage** of the electricity was clearly indicated.
2. Through her training in **CAD/CAM**, she was able to use the computer to assist her with her design.
3. If we want to go home by 5 p.m. and not work overtime, we will need to complete all the **backlog**.
4. Ramon prepared several **batches** of cookies for the party.
5. The company had too many **raw materials** that needed to be processed into the final product.
6. Since the company has installed **robotics**, they have increased their production.
7. Because the lightning had damaged the **transformer** that was connected to the store, there was no electricity for days.
8. The **generators** at the plant were down, which means all production was halted due to no electrical energy.
9. Power plants have **reactors** that are large coils used to introduce reactance into a circuit.
10. Don't **trip** the breaker by putting anything into the wall receptacle.

Answers to Language Skills Self-Check

1. If you plan to graduate by May, you will need to take the following courses this semester: Document Production, OST 210; Machine Transcription, OST 121; and Introduction to Computers, CPT 101.
2. We often pick up a quick lunch at McDonald's, Taco Bell, or Burger King. (No corrections needed.)
3. Gee whiz! I thought I lost my car keys.
4. We often—quite often—think of our needs rather than the needs of others.
5. Our company will be represented at the meeting by Leslie Couric, director; Matt Dillon, marketing manager; and Daniel Scott, supervisor.
6. You must correct that situation immediately—and I mean immediately—before we have a voltage problem!
7. If you prepare—really prepare—for your presentation for the robotics convention, you will be more confident.
8. The following topics will be offered at the seminar: CAD/CAM, robotics, and fiber optics.
9. He has been transferred three times from the following locations: Greenville, South Carolina; Charleston, West Virginia; and Charlotte, North Carolina.
10. We will post high-voltage signs on the front, back, and side of the building.

Student's Name: _____

Instructor's Name: _____

Class: _____

	Date Work Submitted	Grades (Determined by Instructor)
Composition Reinforcement	_____	_____
Collaborative Research	_____	_____
Transcription Exercises	_____	_____
	_____	_____
	_____	_____
	_____	_____

Instructor's Comments Regarding Work or Suggestions for Improvement:

_____

_____

_____

_____

_____

_____

_____

_____

_____

Entertainment, Food, and Restaurant Services

More and more people are dining out today and spending more money on various types of entertainment. An individual needs strong interpersonal skills and a clear perception of customer needs to be successful in these industries. Some management areas in these industries require an associate or bachelor's degree, although some food service managers may have only a high school diploma. The job outlook is expected to grow faster than average in these occupations.

LEARNING OBJECTIVES

After completing all the learning activities in this chapter, you will be able to:

Define and use the word mastery terms presented in this chapter correctly.

Apply the capitalization and parentheses rules presented in this chapter.

Compose five paragraphs in acceptable form utilizing the word mastery terms and language skills presented in this chapter.

Utilize your researching, writing, and communication skills correctly in a collaborative research activity.

Transcribe letters using the block style with open punctuation in acceptable format.

Directions: Learn the definition for each word and how to spell it correctly. Examples of word mastery terms used during the transcription process are given below.

dignitaries

Definition: people who hold a high rank or office

Example: During the election, we saw many dignitaries shaking hands with voters.

quote

Definition: to state a price

Example: When you quote the exact amount for catering my daughter's wedding, I will sign the contract.

buffet

Definition: a meal laid out on a table so that guests may serve themselves

Example: Many restaurants offer a Sunday buffet.

nonrefundable

Definition: no repayment

Example: Because we were told there was a nonrefundable charge, we decided not to purchase the item.

catering

Definition: the act of providing food service

Example: After she worked for a restaurant, Audrey decided to open her own catering service.

deterioration

Definition: damage in quality, function, or condition

Example: The deterioration of the house occurred over the years.

entrée

Definition: the main course of a meal

Example: The entrée was served after the dinner salad had been removed from the table.

filet mignon

Definition: a small, tender round of steak cut from the thick end of a beef tenderloin

Example: Mike always orders filet mignon.

cordon bleu

Definition: a dish cooked with ham and cheese

Example: Chicken cordon bleu is the specialty of the house.

maitre d'

Definition: the head waiter

Example: Our maitre d' directed us to our table.

Directions: Complete each sentence by filling in one of the word mastery terms. You may check your answers at the end of this chapter.

1. There were many _____ at the political fund-raising event.

2. She was told that all purchases were final, and all of the items were _____.

3. _____ of the fabric occurred because of the damage from the sun and heat.

4. What _____ did you choose to eat at the restaurant?

5. My son was hired as the _____ at the country club.

6. One of the most expensive cuts of beef is the _____ _____.

7. When I was planning my daughter's reception, I was wise to get a(n) _____ on the cost of the caterer.

8. Instead of being served individually by the wait staff, everyone was asked to serve themselves from the _____.

9. Before you consider going into the _____ business, be sure you have considered the costs involved in starting a food service.

10. Chicken _____ _____ is an elegant dish to serve for a banquet.

Directions: Review basic grammar and punctuation rules. These rules also appear in the reference manual at the back of your text-workbook.

Rule: Capitalize the names of individuals, buildings, organizations, religious groups, nationalities, and races.

Example: • Bill Clinton, a Democrat from Arkansas, was President of the United States and lived in the White House.

Rule: Capitalize personal titles when they immediately precede individual names. Do not capitalize titles following names except in an address or signature line.

Example: • Marvin Coker, dean of the college, will speak with Mayor Jesse Jordan.

Rule: Days of the week, months of the year, and holidays begin with capital letters.

Example: • We celebrate Thanksgiving Day on Thursday, November 22, this year.

Rule: Use parentheses to enclose figures or letters that mark a series of enumerated elements within a sentence.

Example: • The new business on the agenda will cover: (1) the building proposal, (2) the fund-raising program, and (3) the dues increase.

Directions: Make any corrections in the examples below. Then check your answers at the end of this chapter.

1. We plan to visit the Lincoln Memorial when we visit Washington.

2. Why don't you ask Jacob Lowry, County Treasurer, where the money was spent?

3. Did you see Libby Nelson, Dean of Women, about this issue?

4. We won't be able to visit you on mother's day this year.

5. Let me list the reasons we didn't hire you: you were late for the interview, your resume was not complete, and you were not dressed appropriately for our type of business.

6. The american cancer society is one charity many people support.

7. Angela McDonald, President of our organization, will be the guest speaker.

8. Why don't we plan on eating the easter buffet at the club.

9. Please remember the following procedures: 1. Prepare the dish, 2. Garnish the dish, and present the dish.

10. The republican and democratic parties will hold their national conventions next year.

COMPOSITION REINFORCEMENT

Directions: In the spaces provided, write five paragraphs using the word mastery terms and applying the language skills you have studied. Complete and submit your work for this assignment according to your instructor's directions.

Paragraph 1: Write about a favorite buffet-style restaurant. Use proper capitalization format within the paragraph.

_____

_____

_____

_____

_____

_____

_____

_____

Paragraph 2: Write about a holiday event that might be catered. Be sure to include the name of the holiday and a day and date.

_____

_____

_____

_____

_____

_____

_____

_____

Paragraph 3: Write a paragraph about political officers in your city or state. Use the proper capitalization format for their job titles.

_____

_____

_____

_____

_____

Paragraph 4: What special landmarks or tourist sites have you visited?

_____

_____

_____

_____

_____

_____

Paragraph 5: If you owned a restaurant, what entrées would you include on the menu? Enumerate the items properly within the body of the paragraph.

_____

_____

_____

_____

_____

_____

COLLABORATIVE RESEARCH

Directions: In small groups, work together to answer each numbered item. You may find answers by researching the Internet, newspaper, and library; or you may want to talk with individuals who are actually employed in these fields.

When searching the Internet, you may want to go to **http://www .bls.gov**, click on Publications and Research Papers, click on Occupational Outlook Handbook, and click on the Index to the Handbook for the letter that begins with the word of the field. You also may find information by searching under the name of the field/industry mentioned in the chapter followed by the words *career* or *training*. *Example: restaurant career* or *restaurant training.*

Complete and submit your work for this assignment according to your instructor's directions.

1. Research the employment opportunities for office workers and list the advantages and/or disadvantages of employment in the entertainment, food, or restaurant industries.

_____

_____

_____

_____

_____

_____

_____

2. List the skills or characteristics that are necessary to work in these fields.

_____

_____

_____

_____

_____

_____

_____

3. List the various job titles or positions in these fields.

_____

_____

_____

_____

_____

_____

4. List the salary ranges for positions in these fields.

_____

_____

_____

_____

_____

_____

_____

5. List any additional information you learned during your research.

_____

_____

_____

_____

_____

_____

_____

Directions: Complete all learning activities in this chapter and read all steps before beginning the transcription exercises. In Chapters 7–12, very little punctuation will be dictated on the student's CD. Remember to supply the correct punctuation.

1. Review the format for block style letters with open punctuation in the reference manual.

2. Retrieve the file from the student's CD for each document to be transcribed.
   - For Document 1, open TE9-1, the letterhead for At Your Table Catering.
   - For Document 2, open TE9-2, the letterhead for Chef Pierre.
   - For Document 3, open TE9-3, the letterhead for Kyoto Fantasy Express.
   - For Document 4, open TE9-4, the letterhead for The Baltimore City Club.

3. Remember to use the Save As feature and the name to whom the document was addressed as the filename for each document.

4. Transcribe the four documents from the student's CD in acceptable form using the current date on all correspondence. Use the proper format for block style letters with open punctuation for all four documents.

5. Proofread, spell-check, and submit all four documents to your instructor for approval.

CHAPTER *Checkpoints*

Upon completion of the various learning activities in this chapter, you should be able to meet the objectives listed at the beginning of this chapter. If you feel you cannot answer "yes" to all of the statements listed below, consult your instructor.

Directions: *Place a check mark (✓) in the box for all that apply.*

☐ I can define and use the word mastery terms presented in this chapter.

☐ I can apply the capitalization and parentheses rules presented in this chapter.

☐ I can compose paragraphs in acceptable form utilizing the word mastery terms and language skills presented in this chapter.

☐ I can use my researching, writing, and communication skills correctly.

☐ I can transcribe block style letters with open punctuation in acceptable form.

Answers to Word Mastery Self-Check

1. There were many **dignitaries** at the political fund-raising event.
2. She was told that all purchases were final, and all of the items were **nonrefundable**.
3. **Deterioration** of the fabric occurred because of the damage from the sun and heat.
4. What **entrée** did you choose to eat at the restaurant?
5. My son was hired as the **maitre d'** at the country club.
6. One of the most expensive cuts of beef is the **filet mignon**.
7. When I was planning my daughter's reception, I was wise to get a **quote** on the cost of the caterer.
8. Instead of being served individually by the wait staff, everyone was asked to serve themselves from the **buffet**.
9. Before you consider going into the **catering** business, be sure you have considered the costs involved in starting a food service.
10. Chicken **cordon bleu** is an elegant dish to serve for a banquet.

Answers to Language Skills Self-Check

1. We plan to visit the Lincoln Memorial when we visit Washington. (No corrections needed.)
2. Why don't you ask Jacob Lowry, county treasurer, where the money was spent?
3. Did you see Libby Nelson, dean of women, about this issue?
4. We won't be able to visit you on Mother's Day this year.
5. Let me list the reasons we didn't hire you: (1) you were late for the interview, (2) your resume was not complete, and (3) you were not dressed appropriately for our type of business.
6. The American Cancer Society is one charity many people support.
7. Angela McDonald, president of our organization, will be the guest speaker.
8. Why don't we plan on eating the Easter buffet at the club.
9. Please remember the following procedures: (1) prepare the dish, (2) garnish the dish, and (3) present the dish.
10. The Republican and Democratic Parties will hold their national conventions next year.

Student's Name: _____

Instructor's Name: _____

Class: _____

	Date Work Submitted	Grades (Determined by Instructor)
Composition Reinforcement	_____	_____
Collaborative Research	_____	_____
Transcription Exercises	_____	_____
	_____	_____
	_____	_____
	_____	_____

Instructor's Comments Regarding Work or Suggestions for Improvement:

_____

_____

_____

_____

_____

_____

_____

_____

_____

chapter

Marketing, Retail, and Wholesale Management

The objective of any firm is to market or sell its products or services. If you enjoy selling and like setting and meeting goals, you should consider a career in one of these fields. Many careers in marketing and sales involve a great deal of travel and pressure. A college degree is required for some middle- and upper-management positions. Employment opportunities will grow rapidly, but the competition is expected to be intense.

LEARNING OBJECTIVES

After completing all the learning activities in this chapter, you will be able to:

Define and use the word mastery terms presented in this chapter correctly.

Apply the number and comma rules presented in this chapter.

Compose paragraphs in acceptable form utilizing the word mastery terms and language skills presented in this chapter.

Utilize your researching, writing, and communication skills correctly in a collaborative research activity.

Transcribe letters using the block style with open punctuation and memorandums in acceptable format.

Directions: Learn the definition for each word and how to spell it correctly. Examples of word mastery terms used during the transcription process are given below.

purchase order	*Definition:*	a request or set of instructions according to which goods or services are sold, made, or furnished
	Example:	When the customer submits a purchase order, we can fill the order.
invoice	*Definition:*	a detailed list of goods sold or services provided including the charges and terms of the sale
	Example:	After the bookkeeper received the invoice, she paid the bill.
receipts	*Definition:*	an amount or quantity received
	Example:	When Zackery counted his receipts for his work, he was amazed at the amount of money he had.
customer service	*Definition:*	duties performed professionally with the customer's needs in mind
	Example:	If you don't provide good customer service, your company will lose business.
credit application	*Definition:*	a form that must be completed in order to obtain credit with a company
	Example:	Her credit application was denied because of her poor credit history.
merchandise	*Definition:*	goods or commodities offered for sale
	Example:	Most of the merchandise was stolen.
competitor	*Definition:*	a rival
	Example:	In high school, both sisters were competitors in beauty contests.
promotion	*Definition:*	the act of advertising or marketing a product or service
	Example:	We did not get the type of promotion we felt our book deserved.

| **coupon** | *Definition:* | a detachable portion of a certificate or ticket that entitles the holder to a gift or discount |
| | *Example:* | Many people receive coupons in the mail. |

| **advertisement** | *Definition:* | an announcement promoting a product or service |
| | *Example:* | The advertisement was not in today's newspaper. |

| **quarter** | *Definition:* | one-fourth of a year |
| | *Example:* | The sales staff must meet their goals for the quarter. |

| **redeem** | *Definition:* | to exchange for money or goods |
| | *Example:* | She redeemed her coupons at the grocery store. |

| **profit margin** | *Definition:* | the ratio of gain to the amount of capital invested |
| | *Example:* | Unfortunately, his profit margin was less than he had expected. |

| **overhead** | *Definition:* | the general cost of running a business |
| | *Example:* | Your overhead can be reduced if you find creative ways to save money. |

Directions: Complete each sentence by filling in one of the word mastery terms. You may check your answers at the end of this chapter.

1. Mail the _____ _____ today so we can receive the equipment soon.

2. One _____ _____ telephone tip is to never leave the customer holding the line for more than 30 seconds at a time.

3. The two students were _____ for the most outstanding student award.

4. You can hear many _____ for products on television.

5. The first _____ is usually the busiest for accountants.

6. Before one can receive a credit card, one must complete a(n) _____ _____ that requests various information in order to receive credit.

7. Because the company's _____ was so expensive, the company had to find ways to cut down on some of the costs.

8. Once Janis ordered the crib for her granddaughter, Austin, she received a(n) _____ that lists the amount she owed.

9. Howard and Jane kept all the _____ for the gifts they purchased for Christmas in case they needed to return any of them.

10. The summer _____ was reduced half price in hopes the boutique could sell it quickly and make room for the fall line.

Directions: Review basic grammar and punctuation rules. These rules also appear in the reference manual at the back of your text-workbook.

Rule:	Spell out common fractions appearing alone in ordinary writing. Write mixed numbers as figures.
Examples:	• Over one-fourth of the class was absent yesterday.
	• Use 1 1/2 cups of sugar when making the recipe.

Rule:	Use a comma to set off a nonrestrictive subordinate clause. A nonrestrictive subordinate clause cannot stand alone and is dependent upon the main clause; however, it is not essential to the meaning of the sentence. If the subordinate clause is restrictive and necessary to make the meaning of the sentence clear and complete, do not set it off in commas.
Examples:	• Our new neighbor, who seems very nice, lived in North Dakota before moving to Idaho.
	• All students who have an A average at this point in the semester will not have to take the final exam.

Directions: Make any corrections in the examples below. Then check your answers at the end of this chapter.

1. Jane put one and a third cups of the liquid into the container.

2. We hope that 2/3 of the class will vote for our friend and not for Hayley.

3. If we check the recipe, we will find that it requires 2 1/2 cups of flour.

4. Jessica Cruise who I think is a wonderful actress had the feature role in the movie.

5. The man, who has the fastest car, will win the race.

6. We will have to reduce the merchandise 1/3 to try and move it off the floor.

7. All merchandise, that is purchased during the sale, cannot be returned.

8. The sweater, which was so attractive, did not fit Marie properly.

9. The woman who wore the red vest is the manager.

10. Rita Hanks who is a friendly person will be our new manager.

COMPOSITION REINFORCEMENT

Directions: In the spaces provided, write five paragraphs using the word mastery terms and applying the language skills you have studied. Complete and submit your work for this assignment according to your instructor's directions.

Paragraph 1: Discuss how grocery stores are competitors.

_____

_____

_____

_____

_____

_____

_____

_____

Paragraph 2: What kinds of merchandise might department stores offer?

_____

_____

_____

_____

_____

_____

_____

_____

Paragraph 3: Compose a paragraph to describe a recipe. Use appropriate fractions.

_____
_____
_____
_____
_____
_____

Paragraph 4: Describe an advertisement for a sporting goods store. Use at least two nonrestrictive subordinate clauses.

_____
_____
_____
_____
_____
_____

Paragraph 5: Explain how the terms **redeem** and **coupon** can be used together. Use common fractions in your explanation.

_____
_____
_____
_____
_____
_____

COLLABORATIVE RESEARCH

Directions: In small groups, work together to answer each numbered item. You may find answers by researching the Internet, newspaper, and library; or you may want to talk with individuals who are actually employed in these fields.

When searching the Internet, you may want to go to **http://www.bls.gov**, click on Publications and Research Papers, click on Occupational Outlook Handbook, and click on the Index to the Handbook for the letter that begins with the word of the field. You also may find information by searching under the name of the field/industry mentioned in the chapter followed by the words *career* or *training. Example: marketing career* or *marketing training.*

Complete and submit your work for this assignment according to your instructor's directions.

1. Research the employment opportunities for office workers and list the advantages and/or disadvantages of employment in marketing, retail, and wholesale management.

_____

_____

_____

_____

_____

_____

_____

2. List the skills or characteristics that are necessary to work in these fields.

_____

_____

_____

_____

_____

_____

_____

_____

3. List the various job titles or positions in these fields.

_____

_____

_____

_____

_____

_____

4. List the salary ranges for positions in these fields.

_____

_____

_____

_____

_____

_____

5. List any additional information you learned during your research.

_____

_____

_____

_____

_____

_____

TRANSCRIPTION EXERCISES

Directions: Complete all learning activities in this chapter and read all steps before beginning the transcription exercises. In Chapters 7–12, very little punctuation will be dictated on the student's CD. Remember to supply the correct punctuation.

1. Review the format for block style letters with open punctuation and interoffice memorandums in the reference manual.

2. Retrieve the file from the student's CD for each document to be transcribed.
   - For Document 1, open TE10-1, the letterhead for Mom and Pop's Texan Apparel.
   - For Document 2, open TE10-2, the letterhead for Town and Country Casuals.

   - For Document 3, open TE10-3, the letterhead for Omaha Wholesale Grocery.
   - For Document 4, open TE10-4, the letterhead for Barton's Retail.

3. Remember to use the Save As feature and use the name of the individual to whom the document was addressed as the filename for each document.

4. Transcribe the four documents from the student's CD in acceptable form using the current date on all correspondence. Use the proper format for interoffice memorandums for Documents 1 and 4; use the proper format for block style letters with open punctuation for Documents 2 and 3.

5. Proofread, spell-check, and submit all four documents to your instructor for approval.

CHAPTER *Checkpoints*

Upon completion of the various learning activities in this chapter, you should be able to meet the objectives listed at the beginning of this chapter. If you feel you cannot answer "yes" to all of the statements listed below, consult your instructor.

Directions: *Place a check mark (✔) in the box for all that apply.*

☐ I can define and use the word mastery terms presented in this chapter.

☐ I can apply the number and comma rules presented in this chapter.

☐ I can compose paragraphs in acceptable form utilizing the word mastery terms and language skills presented in this chapter.

☐ I can use my researching, writing, and communication skills correctly.

☐ I can transcribe block style letters and memorandums in acceptable form.

Answers to Word Mastery Self-Check

1. Mail the **purchase order** today so we can receive the equipment soon.
2. One **customer service** telephone tip is to never leave the customer holding the line for more than 30 seconds at a time.
3. The two students were **competitors** for the most outstanding student award.
4. You can hear many **advertisements** for products on television.
5. The first **quarter** is usually the busiest for accountants.
6. Before one can receive a credit card, one must complete a **credit application** that requests various information in order to receive credit.
7. Because the company's **overhead** was so expensive, the company had to find ways to cut down on some of the costs.
8. Once Janis ordered the crib for her granddaughter, Austin, she received an **invoice** that lists the amount she owed.
9. Howard and Jane kept all the **receipts** for the gifts they purchased for Christmas in case they needed to return any of them.
10. The summer **merchandise** was reduced half price in hopes the boutique could sell it quickly and make room for the fall line.

Answers to Language Skills Self-Check

1. Jane put 1 1/3 cups of the liquid into the container.
2. We hope that two-thirds of the class will vote for our friend and not for Hayley.
3. If we check the recipe, we will find that it requires 2 1/2 cups of flour. (No corrections needed.)
4. Jessica Cruise, who I think is a wonderful actress, had the feature role in the movie.
5. The man who has the fastest car will win the race.
6. We will have to reduce the merchandise one-third to try and move it off the floor.
7. All merchandise that is purchased during the sale cannot be returned.
8. The sweater, which was so attractive, did not fit Marie properly. (No corrections needed.)
9. The woman who wore the red vest is the manager. (No corrections needed.)
10. Rita Hanks, who is a friendly person, will be our new manager.

Student's Name: _____

Instructor's Name: _____

Class: _____

	Date Work Submitted	Grades (Determined by Instructor)
Composition Reinforcement	_____	_____
Collaborative Research	_____	_____
Transcription Exercises	_____	_____
	_____	_____
	_____	_____
	_____	_____

Instructor's Comments Regarding Work or Suggestions for Improvement:

_____

_____

_____

_____

_____

_____

_____

_____

chapter

Travel, Tourism, and Hotel Services

*E*mployment opportunities in these industries may be found in travel agencies, motels, hotels, resorts, and airports. Some positions have minimal entry requirements; other positions require postsecondary training or college degrees. Although these industries can be exciting and seem glamorous, long work hours and odd shifts are usually required. High stress levels are common in many positions in these industries.

LEARNING OBJECTIVES

After completing all the learning activities in this chapter, you will be able to:

Define and use the word mastery terms presented in this chapter correctly.

Apply the parentheses and capitalization rules presented in this chapter.

Compose paragraphs in acceptable form utilizing the word mastery terms and language skills presented in this chapter.

Utilize your researching, writing, and communication skills correctly in a collaborative research activity.

Transcribe letters in block style with open punctuation in acceptable form.

Directions: Learn the definition for each word and how to spell it correctly. Examples of word mastery terms used during the transcription process are given below.

arrangements

Definition: preparations

Example: Last-minute arrangements had to be made before the wedding.

conference

Definition: a meeting for consultation or discussion

Example: After the conference, all the participants knew what the company expected them to achieve in the next year.

accommodations

Definition: lodging arrangements

Example: Because no accommodations had been arranged, they did not have a room for the night.

confirmed

Definition: verified

Example: Lauren confirmed her appointment with her physician.

ninety

Definition: ten times nine

Example: She had lived ninety years before she became ill.

occupancy

Definition: amount of space allowed

Example: The maximum occupancy for the room was 125 people.

customized

Definition: made to individual orders

Example: After his measurements were taken, the tailor customized the suit for him.

inquiry

Definition: a question

Example: Please send your inquiry about this position to the supervisor.

authentic

Definition: genuine or real

Example: Her jewelry was not authentic.

itinerary

Definition: a detailed plan for a trip or visit

Example: If you would like a copy of Ivan's itinerary so you can contact him while he is gone, please let me know.

attractions	*Definition:*	people or things that draw attention
	Example:	When you are on your vacation, be sure to see as many attractions as you can.
questionnaire	*Definition:*	a list of questions submitted for replies that can be analyzed
	Example:	When you complete the enclosed questionnaire, send it to us immediately.
bed and breakfast inn	*Definition:*	accommodations other than a hotel/motel that provide lodging and the morning meal for guests
	Example:	Some people find bed and breakfast inns more intimate than the larger hotel and motel chains.
cuisine	*Definition:*	food
	Example:	The South is known for having wonderful cuisine.
pedicure	*Definition:*	professional treatment or care of the feet
	Example:	Wanda enjoyed the pedicure she received from the salon.
manicure	*Definition:*	professional treatment or care of the hands
	Example:	After seeing how attractive her hands looked, Savita decided to have a manicure once a week.
reservation	*Definition:*	secured arrangements
	Example:	Be sure you make your reservation for the business trip.
confirmation	*Definition:*	valid or proven
	Example:	She did not ask for her confirmation number.

Directions: Complete each sentence by filling in one of the word mastery terms. You may check your answers at the end of this chapter.

1. He hoped he could attend the _____ that was to be held in North Dakota.

2. Because of fire codes, the _____ of the elevator was limited to ten people.

3. Your _____ regarding this matter will be directed to our manager.

4. Yoko kept a copy of her employer's _____ available while her employer was traveling.

5. A(n) _____ can provide valuable feedback to researchers.

6. Be sure you made your _____ for your hotel room.

7. Many people prefer to stay at a(n) _____ _____ _____ _____ instead of some of the large hotel and motel chains.

8. Many restaurants are known for their fine _____.

9. Because Rico did not like the _____ the hotel desk clerk made for him, he requested another room.

10. Marbella wanted to add a(n) _____ to her day at the spa when she finished having her manicure.

Directions: Review basic grammar and punctuation rules. These rules also appear in the reference manual at the back of your text-workbook.

Rule: Use parentheses to enclose figures verifying a number that is spelled out.

Example:
- I owe him twenty-five dollars ($25).

Rule: Capitalize the proper names of states, motels and hotels, businesses, cultural, or entertainment facilities. Common names are not capitalized.

Examples:
- I will visit Idaho and stay at the Idaho Inn while I attend the Idaho State Fair.
- After visiting the city park in his home state, Shane spent the night at the hotel.

Directions: Insert parentheses as needed and provide the correct capitalization in the examples below. Then check your answers at the end of this chapter.

1. Harrison hoped his grandmother would send him twenty dollars ($20) for his birthday.

2. I plan to spend thirty dollars $30 on his wedding gift.

3. Don't you want to go to the Baseball Stadium this afternoon?

4. After seeing Yankee Stadium, I knew I wanted to be a baseball player.

5. Let's visit the City Zoo next month.

6. If you want to reserve the room, the rate will be seventy dollars ($70) per night.

7. We will need to visit the Washington Memorial when we are in Washington.

8. Does her son work at the state park?

9. Of course, we will visit the Florida State Park when we go on vacation.

10. We don't usually enjoy eating at seafood restaurants, but we did enjoy eating at Captain Eddie's Seafood Palace.

COMPOSITION REINFORCEMENT

Directions: In the spaces provided, write five paragraphs using the word mastery terms and applying the language skills you have studied. Complete and submit your work for this assignment according to your instructor's directions.

Paragraph 1: Compose a paragraph confirming a reservation. Use a sentence with parentheses to explain a dollar amount.

_____

_____

_____

_____

_____

_____

_____

_____

Paragraph 2: List questions in paragraph form that might be included on a questionnaire for possible vacation interests.

_____

_____

_____

_____

_____

_____

_____

_____

Paragraph 3: Explain the difference between **manicure** and **pedicure**. Use the proper names of salons as well as general names in the body of the paragraph.

_____

_____

_____

_____

_____

_____

Paragraph 4: Discuss a plan for a conference and its suggested itinerary.

_____

_____

_____

_____

_____

_____

Paragraph 5: Compose a paragraph discussing your favorite cuisine. Use the language skills rules from this chapter in the body of the paragraph.

_____

_____

_____

_____

_____

_____

_____

COLLABORATIVE RESEARCH

Directions: In small groups, work together to answer each numbered item. You may find answers by researching the Internet, newspaper, and library; or you may want to talk with individuals who are actually employed in these fields.

When searching the Internet, you may want to go to **http://www .bls.gov**, click on Publications and Research Papers, click on Occupational Outlook Handbook, and click on the Index to the Handbook for the letter that begins with the word of the field. You also may find information by searching under the name of the field/industry mentioned in the chapter followed by the words *career* or *training*. *Example: travel career* or *travel training.*

Complete and submit your work for this assignment according to your instructor's directions.

1. Research the employment opportunities for office workers and list the advantages and/or disadvantages of employment in travel, tourism, and hotel services.

_____

_____

_____

_____

_____

_____

_____

2. List the skills or characteristics that are necessary to work in these fields.

_____

_____

_____

_____

_____

_____

_____

_____

3. List the various job titles or positions in these fields.

_____

_____

_____

_____

_____

_____

4. List the salary ranges for positions in these fields.

_____

_____

_____

_____

_____

_____

_____

5. List any additional information you learned during your research.

_____

_____

_____

_____

_____

_____

Directions: Complete all learning activities in this chapter and read all steps before beginning the transcription exercises. In Chapters 7–12, very little punctuation will be dictated on the student's CD. Remember to supply the correct punctuation.

1. Review the format for a block letter with open punctuation in the reference manual.

2. Retrieve the file from the student's CD for each document to be transcribed.
   - For Document 1, open TE11-1, the letterhead for Tampa Tour Company.
   - For Document 2, open TE11-2, the letterhead for Wyoming Travel Group.

   - For Document 3, open TE11-3, the letterhead for The Hide-Away.
   - For Document 4, open TE11-4, the letterhead for Peach State Travel Agency.

3. Remember to use the Save As feature and the name of the individual to whom the document was addressed as the filename for each document.

4. Transcribe all four documents on the student's CD in acceptable form using the current date. Use the proper format for block style letters with open punctuation for all four documents.

5. Proofread, spell-check, and submit all four documents to your instructor for approval.

CHAPTER *Checkpoints*

Upon completion of the various learning activities in this chapter, you should be able to meet the objectives listed at the beginning of this chapter. If you feel you cannot answer "yes" to all of the statements listed below, consult your instructor.

Directions: *Place a check mark (✓) in the box for all that apply.*

☐ I can define and use the word mastery terms presented in this chapter.

☐ I can apply the parentheses and capitalization rules presented in this chapter.

☐ I can compose paragraphs in acceptable form utilizing the word mastery terms and language skills presented in this chapter.

☐ I can use my researching, writing, and communication skills correctly.

☐ I can transcribe letters using block style with open punctuation in acceptable form.

Answers to Word Mastery Self-Check

1. He hoped he could attend the **conference** that was to be held in North Dakota.
2. Because of fire codes, the **occupancy** of the elevator was limited to ten people.
3. Your **inquiry** regarding this matter will be directed to our manager.
4. Yoko kept a copy of her employer's **itinerary** available while her employer was traveling.
5. A **questionnaire** can provide valuable feedback to researchers.
6. Be sure you made your **reservation** for your hotel room.
7. Many people prefer to stay at a **bed and breakfast inn** instead of some of the large hotel and motel chains.
8. Many restaurants are known for their fine **cuisine.**
9. Because Rico did not like the **accommodations** the hotel desk clerk made for him, he requested another room.
10. Marbella wanted to add a **pedicure** to her day at the spa when she finished having her manicure.

Answers to Language Skills Self-Check

1. Harrison hoped his grandmother would send him twenty dollars ($20) for his birthday. (No corrections needed.)
2. I plan to spend thirty dollars ($30) on his wedding gift.
3. Don't you want to go to the baseball stadium this afternoon?
4. After seeing Yankee Stadium, I knew I wanted to be a baseball player. (No corrections needed.)
5. Let's visit the city zoo next month.
6. If you want to reserve the room, the rate will be seventy dollars ($70) per night. (No corrections needed.)
7. We will need to visit the Washington Memorial when we are in Washington. (No corrections needed.)
8. Does her son work at the state park? (No corrections needed.)
9. Of course, we will visit the Florida State Park when we go on vacation. (No corrections needed.)
10. We don't usually enjoy eating at seafood restaurants, but we did enjoy eating at Captain Eddie's Seafood Palace. (No corrections needed.)

Student's Name: _____

Instructor's Name: _____

Class: _____

	Date Work Submitted	Grades (Determined by Instructor)
Composition Reinforcement	_____	_____
Collaborative Research	_____	_____
Transcription Exercises	_____	_____
	_____	_____
	_____	_____
	_____	_____

Instructor's Comments Regarding Work or Suggestions for Improvement:

_____

_____

_____

_____

_____

_____

_____

_____

_____

chapter

Airline, Automotive, and Trucking

Within these industries, there are many types of positions from which you may choose. Sales staff, customer service representatives, mechanics, and operators are among some of the diverse positions that may interest you. Although some positions only require a high school diploma, other positions require postsecondary or college training. Still, others require specialized training and licensing. These traffic and transportation industries must meet state and federal regulations.

LEARNING OBJECTIVES

After completing all the learning activities in this chapter, you will be able to:

Define and use the word mastery terms presented in this chapter correctly.

Apply the hyphenation and capitalization rules presented in this chapter.

Compose paragraphs in acceptable form utilizing the word mastery terms and language skills presented in this chapter.

Utilize your researching, writing, and communication skills correctly in a collaborative research activity.

Transcribe tables, memos, and letters in block style with open punctuation in acceptable form.

Directions: Learn the definition for each word and how to spell it correctly. Examples of word mastery terms used during the transcription process are given below.

boarding	*Definition:*	the act of entering a plane, ship, or train
	Example:	As she was boarding the plane, she fell and broke her leg.
destination	*Definition:*	the place to which a person or thing travels or is sent
	Example:	When she planned her trip, her final destination was Alaska.
charter	*Definition:*	reserve for a special purpose
	Example:	The team wanted to fly by charter service rather than commercial service.
interstate	*Definition:*	involving movement between states
	Example:	The United States government now allows interstate commerce.
license	*Definition:*	a formal permission from a constituted authority to do a special thing
	Example:	Rebecca was excited when she received her driver's license.
analysis	*Definition:*	the process of studying the nature of something
	Example:	After much analysis, the company decided to cut labor costs.
replenish	*Definition:*	to make full or complete again
	Example:	After most of the office supplies were used, the office professional wanted to replenish the supply cabinet.
inventory	*Definition:*	merchandise, materials, or stock on hand
	Example:	Much of the company's inventory was damaged in the fire.
vehicles	*Definition:*	equipment used to move or carry something
	Example:	Several vehicles were stolen from the parking lot.
model	*Definition:*	the type of vehicle such as two-door or four-door
	Example:	Because they had several children, the couple decided on the four-door model rather than the two-door.

make	*Definition:*	the manufacturer of the vehicle such as Ford or Dodge
	Example:	He indicated that the make of his car is a BMW.
inspection	*Definition:*	examination
	Example:	We no longer have inspection stickers on our automobiles.
log	*Definition:*	various detailed records of the operation of a vehicle
	Example:	Because he had lost his log, Jim could not complete his travel expense report.
dispatched	*Definition:*	to send off with efficiency
	Example:	He dispatched the taxi immediately.

Directions: Complete each sentence by filling in one of the word mastery terms. You may check your answers at the end of this chapter.

1. The couple left for their honeymoon; however, no one knew their actual _____.

2. You will need to _____ the paper in your printer.

3. As we unpacked the _____, we noticed that some of the equipment had been lost.

4. Upon further _____, Jolene discovered that the table had been damaged.

5. He _____ the ambulance as soon as he received the 911 call.

6. Many _____ were on the car lot for sale.

7. When people purchase automobiles, they want to select the _____ that suits their family's needs.

8. If your parents drove a certain _____ of automobile, you probably tend to purchase from the same manufacturer.

9. Drivers have to keep a(n) _____ of the mileage they complete.

10. Driving on the _____ can be dangerous.

Directions: Review basic grammar and punctuation rules. These rules also appear in the reference manual at the back of your text-workbook.

Rule: Use a hyphen to show passage of time, except when used with *from* or *between*.

Examples:
- Boarding time is scheduled for 1:30–2:00 p.m.
- People holding tickets may board the ferry between 1:30 and 2:00 p.m.
- Juan lived in Chicago from 1998 to 1999.

Rule: Capitalize proper names of cities, states, rivers, mountains, etc. Common nouns are not capitalized.

Examples:
- Mount Waialeala is on Kauai in the Hawaiian Islands.
- We hope to raft many rivers and to climb several mountains in the western states this summer.

Rule: Capitalize compass directions when they are used to name a particular part of the country. Do not capitalize these words when they merely indicate a general location or direction.

Example:
- To view the best colors in the East, travel north through the state on I-91.

Directions: Provide the correct hyphenation and capitalization in the examples below. Then check your answers at the end of this chapter.

1. We will hold our meeting from 1:30–3:30 p.m.

2. We can see you between 9:00 and 10:30 a.m. today.

3. Don't you think the people in the south are friendly?

4. Her office faces West; his office faces East.

5. She stopped by the Mississippi river to see the steamboats.

6. The flight was 3:00 p.m. to 4:30 p.m.

7. We drove past the state line.

8. Marcela drove North to see her family.

9. Rico lived in the south all his life.

10. Don't you think we should visit the State Capital on our next road trip?

COMPOSITION REINFORCEMENT

Directions: In the spaces provided, write five paragraphs using the word mastery terms and applying the language skills you have studied. Complete and submit your work for this assignment according to your instructor's directions.

Paragraph 1: Plan a trip to a favorite destination. Include a schedule with hyphenated times.

_____

_____

_____

_____

_____

_____

_____

Paragraph 2: What kinds of inventory would be included at an automobile dealership?

_____

_____

_____

_____

_____

_____

_____

_____

Paragraph 3: Compose a possible log for a business trip.

_____

_____

_____

_____

_____

_____

Paragraph 4: Explain the term **interstate** and use compass directions in the body of the paragraph.

_____

_____

_____

_____

_____

_____

_____

Paragraph 5: What is a **charter** flight? Use proper and common nouns in your definition.

_____

_____

_____

_____

_____

_____

_____

COLLABORATIVE RESEARCH

Directions: In small groups, work together to answer each numbered item. You may find answers by researching the Internet, newspaper, and library; or you may want to talk with individuals who are actually employed in these fields.

When searching the Internet, you may want to go to **http://www .bls.gov**, click on Publications and Research Papers, click on Occupational Outlook Handbook, and click on the Index to the Handbook for the letter that begins with the word of the field. You also may find information by searching under the name of the field/industry mentioned in the chapter followed by the words *career* or *training*. *Example: trucking career* or *trucking training.*

Complete and submit your work for this assignment according to your instructor's directions.

1. Research the employment opportunities for office workers and list the advantages and/or disadvantages of employment in the airline, automotive, or trucking industries.

_____

_____

_____

_____

_____

_____

_____

2. List the skills or characteristics that are necessary to work in these industries.

_____

_____

_____

_____

_____

_____

_____

3. List the various job titles or positions in these industries.

_____

_____

_____

_____

_____

_____

_____

4. List the salary ranges for positions in these industries.

_____

_____

_____

_____

_____

_____

_____

_____

5. List any additional information you learned during your research.

_____

_____

_____

_____

_____

_____

_____

_____

Directions: Complete all learning activities in this chapter and read all steps before beginning the transcription exercises. In Chapters 7–12, very little punctuation will be dictated on the student's CD. Remember to supply the correct punctuation.

1. Review the format for tables, block letters with open punctuation, and memorandums in the reference manual.

2. Retrieve the file from the student's CD for each document to be transcribed.
   - Print Document 1 on plain paper.
   - For Document 2, open TE12-2, the letterhead for Washington Airlines.

   - For Document 3, open TE12-3, the letterhead for Mendez Rentals.
   - For Document 4, open TE12-4, the letterhead for Fitzgerald Trucking Lines.

3. For Documents 2-4, remember to use the Save As feature and the name of the individual to whom the document was addressed as the filename.

4. Transcribe all four documents on the student's CD in acceptable form using the current date. Use the proper format for tables for Document 1; use the proper format for block style letters with open punctuation for Documents 2 and 3; use the proper format for interoffice memorandums for Document 4.

5. Proofread, spell-check, and submit all four documents to your instructor for approval.

CHAPTER *Checkpoints*

Upon completion of the various learning activities in this chapter, you should be able to meet the objectives listed at the beginning of this chapter. If you feel you cannot answer "yes" to all of the statements listed below, consult your instructor.

Directions: *Place a check mark (✔) in the box for all that apply.*

- ☐ I can define and use the word mastery terms presented in this chapter.

- ☐ I can apply the hyphenation and capitalization rules presented in this chapter.

- ☐ I can compose paragraphs in acceptable form utilizing the word mastery terms and language skills presented in this chapter.

- ☐ I can use my researching, writing, and communication skills correctly.

- ☐ I can transcribe tables, block letters with open punctuation, and memorandums in acceptable form.

Answers to Word Mastery Self-Check

1. The couple left for their honeymoon; however, no one knew their actual **destination**.
2. You will need to **replenish** the paper in your printer.
3. As we unpacked the **inventory**, we noticed that some of the equipment had been lost.
4. Upon further **inspection**, Jolene discovered that the table had been damaged.
5. He **dispatched** the ambulance as soon as he received the 911 call.
6. Many **vehicles** were on the car lot for sale.
7. When people purchase automobiles, they want to select the **model** that suits their family's needs.
8. If your parents drove a certain **make** of automobile, you probably tend to purchase from the same manufacturer.
9. Drivers have to keep a **log** of the mileage they complete.
10. Driving on the **interstate** can be dangerous.

Answers to Language Skills Self-Check

1. We will hold our meeting from 1:30 to 3:30 p.m.
2. We can see you between 9:00 and 10:30 a.m. today. (No corrections needed.)
3. Don't you think the people in the South are friendly?
4. Her office faces west; his office faces east.
5. She stopped by the Mississippi River to see the steamboats.
6. The flight was 3:00 p.m.–4:30 p.m.
7. We drove past the state line. (No corrections needed.)
8. Marcela drove north to see her family.
9. Rico lived in the South all his life.
10. Don't you think we should visit the state capital on our next road trip?

After you have completed Chapter 12, you should complete the proofreading assignment on the following page to help prepare yourself for the tests for Part 2. Follow your instructor's guidelines for completing this assignment. Take the written test and transcription test for Part 2 before proceeding to Chapter 13.

PROOFREADING ASSIGNMENT

Directions: This assignment should be completed following your instructor's guidelines. You may need to refer to the listing of the most commonly misspelled words as well as the listing of the most frequently misused words in business and industry. Both of these lists are located in your text-workbook. Refer to the list of proofreading marks in your text-workbook to be sure that you use the correct proofreading mark to indicate all errors that you find.

CARREER CHOICES

There are many careers fields from which you may chose. In the six chapters in Part 1 you learned about the advertising, journalism and publishing fields, education, government, and public service fields, real estate, appraising, and property managment fields, accounnting, auditing, and financial planning fields, and banking financial management, and consumer credit fields. In the 6 chapters in Part 2 you studied the following fields and industries insurance field, engineering, industrial, and manufacturing fields, entertainment, food, and restaurant services, marketing, retail, and wholesale management, travel, tourism, and hotel service, and the airline, automotive, and trucking industry.

The next part in this text-workbook will pertain to the legal and medical fields. There is a strong need for machine transcriptionist in these too specialty areas.

Student's Name: _____

Instructor's Name: _____

Class: _____

	Date Work Submitted	Grades (Determined by Instructor)
Composition Reinforcement	_____	_____
Collaborative Research	_____	_____
Transcription Exercises	_____	_____
	_____	_____
	_____	_____
	_____	_____
Proofreading Assignment	_____	_____

Instructor's Comments Regarding Work or Suggestions for Improvement:

_____

_____

_____

_____

_____

_____

Part 3

Advanced Machine Transcription—Legal and Medical

chapter

Contingency Fee Agreement, Certificate of Notary, and Probate Court Form

The legal system affects many aspects of our lives because laws define the rules of society. The legal system can be divided into two areas, private law and public law. Private law (also called civil law) governs the relationships among members of a community. Public law is concerned with matters such as constitutional, administrative, and criminal law. Law firms can be small or large; some large law firms have several offices in various locations. Machine transcription is used heavily within the legal community. Therefore, the next four chapters of this text-workbook will be directed to this specialty.

Since law is concerned with defining what is and is not permissible in society, the language and style of legal documents are quite formal. Care must be taken with all information presented in a legal context. Because Chapters 13–20 are considered the advanced phase of your machine transcription training, you will be asked to review some language skills from previous chapters and apply them within these chapters in addition to the language skills presented in each chapter. A summary of all the language skills rules is in the reference section.

LEARNING OBJECTIVES

After completing all the learning activities in this chapter, you will be able to:

Define and use the word mastery terms presented in this chapter correctly.

Apply the capitalization and word division rules presented in this chapter.

Compose paragraphs in acceptable form utilizing the word mastery terms and language skills presented in this chapter and other punctuation and grammar rules that were presented in earlier chapters and in the reference manual.

Utilize your researching, writing, and communication skills correctly in a collaborative research activity.

Transcribe legal documents in acceptable form.

Directions: Learn the definition for each word and how to spell it correctly. Examples of word mastery terms used during the transcription process are given below.

contingency fee

Definition: an attorney's fee based on a percentage of the amount of money recovered in a legal action

Example: The lawyer agreed to accept a contingency fee rather than a fee based on an hourly rate.

attorney

Definition: generally, someone qualified and given the authority to act in another's behalf; specifically, a lawyer

Example: Because he was being sued by the motorist who hit him, Ramon asked his attorney to represent him in the case.

Certificate of Notary

Definition: a document containing the facts sworn to be true before someone legally authorized to certify the document

Example: When Elena signed the Certificate of Notary, she swore that she had told the truth.

Notary Public

Definition: someone legally authorized to administer oaths and certify documents

Example: Jarmaine presented the document to be signed to the Notary Public.

acknowledged

Definition: to have declared or admitted that something is true

Example: Rudie acknowledged that Linda's statement was true.

seal

Definition: a pledge or promise

Example: A written or spoken seal secures a document in an abstract manner just as wax or glue secures a document in a physical manner.

instrument

Definition: any formal legal document

Example: The Certificate of Notary is an example of an instrument used within our legal system.

testimony

Definition: evidence presented by a witness under oath in a court of law

Example: Before her case was settled, Patty was prepared to give testimony.

probate	*Definition:*	to prove legally that a will is valid or genuine
	Example:	Charlene's will has been admitted into probate court.
will	*Definition:*	the legal declaration for the distribution of one's property and possessions after death
	Example:	In her will, Alice's mother left her brother everything except the house and the land.
decedent	*Definition:*	a person who has died
	Example:	Mail continued to arrive, addressed to the decedent, in the months following the funeral.
witnesses	*Definition:*	observing and acknowledging in writing the execution of an instrument
	Example:	The attorney asked Emily and her brother to be witnesses to the signing of the will.

Directions: Complete each sentence by filling in one of the word mastery terms. You may check your answers at the end of this chapter.

1. She went to see her _____ for legal advice.

2. Greg _____ yesterday that the person who had testified did not give all the facts in the case.

3. Because his _____ was necessary in the case, he was required to be present the day of the trial.

4. Be sure that we have our _____ kept in a safe place where they can easily be located in case of death.

5. The _____ had no living relatives.

6. Some legal documents need to have the signature of a(n) _____ _____ to certify the documents.

7. We will have to call several _____ to the stand to state what they observed during the accident.

8. When someone dies, his/her will must go through _____ to prove it is valid.

9. Rather than charging his client an hourly rate, Jonathan Carroll and his client settled on a(n) _____ _____ .

10. A Contingency Fee Agreement is a legal document or _____ used in our legal system.

Directions: Review basic grammar and punctuation rules. These rules also appear in the reference manual.

Rule:	When keying a legal document, use all capital letters for the names of the parties to a legal agreement.
Example:	• The plaintiff, SHIRLEY NEELY, is a resident of the State of Colorado. (Sentence in a legal document.)

Rule:	Do not divide a one-syllable word.
Example:	• bound shipped wrapped

Rule:	Divide a word between syllables if you can leave at least three characters on the first line and carry three characters to the next line. (A mark of punctuation such as a hyphen, a comma, or a period may count as one of the characters.)
Examples:	• thought-ful
	• re-ceive (three characters *r*, *e*, and the hyphen on one line and more than three characters carried to the next line)
	• anoth-er (cannot be divided at this point because three characters are not carried to the next line; an-other would be acceptable)
	• a-way (cannot be divided because you cannot place at least three characters on the first line)

Directions: These examples include a review of language skills presented in the previous chapters. You may want to refer to the reference manual in the back of this student text-workbook for a review before completing these examples.

Make any corrections in the following sentences. Then check your answers at the end of this chapter.

1. Jeremy Johnson, furnished the correct information regarding the rental of the premises. (Sentence in a legal document.)

2. The details of her divorce were not given to me.

3. The attorney of course kept his client informed of all aspects of the case.

4. Carla gave Fred Ledford her attorney the information he had requested.

5. If Phoebe seeks legal advice regarding the lawsuit she will be extremely wise.

6. The cost of the various procedures were never explained.

7. We will however be responsible for paying the contingency fee for legal counsel.

8. Don't you want to ask your client Linda Rowan if she has any other pertinent information regarding the case.

9. When you have all the documentation to be keyed into the computer give it to our legal secretary Sarah Buck.

10. JENNIFER NELSON is the plaintiff in the case. (Sentence in a legal document.)

Indicate the correct place to divide the words listed below. Then check your answers at the end of this chapter.

strained   enough   stormy   disturb

COMPOSITION REINFORCEMENT

Directions: In the spaces provided, compose a paragraph using the word mastery terms and applying the language skills you have studied. Complete and submit your work for this assignment according to your instructor's directions.

Paragraph 1: Explain how **Certificate of Notary** and **Notary Public** are related.

_____

_____

_____

_____

_____

_____

_____

_____

Paragraph 2: Show that you understand the word **acknowledged**.

_____

_____

_____

_____

_____

_____

_____

_____

Paragraph 3: Briefly explain a possible legal case and show how the name of a person would appear in a legal document.

_____

_____

_____

_____

_____

_____

Paragraph 4: Explain how the terms **witness** and **testimony** are related.

_____

_____

_____

_____

_____

_____

Paragraph 5: Explain some responsibilities of an attorney using some of the word mastery terms. Show an understanding of word division.

_____

_____

_____

_____

_____

_____

_____

COLLABORATIVE RESEARCH

Directions: In small groups, work together to answer each numbered item. You may find answers by researching the Internet, newspaper, and library; or you may want to talk with individuals who are actually employed in this field.

When searching the Internet, you may want to go to **http://www .bls.gov**, click on Publications and Research Papers, click on Occupational Outlook Handbook, and click on the Index to the Handbook for the letter that begins with the word of the field. You also may find information by searching under the name of the field/industry mentioned in the chapter followed by the words *career* or *training. Example: legal career* or *legal training.*

Complete and submit your work for this assignment according to your instructor's directions.

1. Research the employment opportunities for office workers and list the advantages and/or disadvantages of employment in the legal profession.

_____

_____

_____

_____

_____

_____

_____

_____

2. List the skills or characteristics that are necessary to work in this field.

_____

_____

_____

_____

_____

_____

_____

3. List the various job titles or positions in this field.

_____

_____

_____

_____

_____

_____

4. List the salary ranges for positions in this field.

_____

_____

_____

_____

_____

_____

5. List any additional information you learned during your research.

_____

_____

_____

_____

_____

_____

TRANSCRIPTION EXERCISES

Directions: Complete all learning activities in this chapter and read all steps before beginning the transcription exercises.

1. Review the format for legal documents in the reference manual.

2. Retrieve the file from the student CD for each document to be transcribed.
   - For Document 1, open TE13-1, the Contingency Fee Agreement.
   - Print Document 2, Certificate of Notary, on plain paper.
   - For Document 3, open TE13-3, the Probate Court form.

3. For Documents 1 and 3, remember to use the Save As feature and an appropriate filename.

4. In Documents 1 and 3, you will be required to key the variable information into the underlined spaces in the file. Remove the underlines after you have supplied the information. *Be sure to read the entire document after you have supplied the information dictated so you are familiar with* *the content of the documents.*

5. Transcribe all the legal documents on the CD in acceptable form using the current date unless another date is given.

6. Proofread, spell-check, and submit all documents to your instructor for approval.

CHAPTER *Checkpoints*

Upon completion of the various learning activities in this chapter, you should be able to meet the objectives listed at the beginning of this chapter. If you feel you cannot answer "yes" to all of the statements listed below, consult your instructor.

Directions: *Place a check mark (✓) in the box for all that apply.*

☐ I can define and use the word mastery terms presented in this chapter.

☐ I can apply the capitalization and word division rules presented in this chapter and other punctuation and grammar rules that are presented in earlier chapters and in the reference manual.

☐ I can compose paragraphs in acceptable form utilizing the word mastery terms and language skills presented in this chapter.

☐ I can use my researching, writing, and communication skills correctly.

☐ I can transcribe legal documents in acceptable form.

Answers to Word Mastery Self-Check

1. She went to see her **attorney** for legal advice.
2. Greg **acknowledged** yesterday that the person who had testified did not give all the facts in the case.
3. Because his **testimony** was necessary in the case, he was required to be present the day of the trial.
4. Be sure that we have our **wills** kept in a safe place where they can easily be located in case of death.
5. The **decedent** had no living relatives.
6. Some legal documents need to have the signature of a **notary public** to certify the documents.
7. We will have to call several **witnesses** to the stand to state what they observed during the accident.
8. When someone dies, his/her will must go through **probate** to prove it is valid.
9. Rather than charging his client an hourly rate, Jonathan Carroll and his client settled on a **contingency fee**.
10. A Contingency Fee Agreement is a legal document or **instrument** used in our legal system.

Answers to Language Skills Self-Check

1. JEREMY JOHNSON furnished the correct information regarding the rental of the premises. (Sentence from a legal document.)
2. The details of her divorce were not given to me. (No corrections needed.)
3. The attorney, of course, kept his client informed of all aspects of the case.
4. Carla gave Fred Ledford, her attorney, the information he had requested.
5. If Phoebe seeks legal advice regarding the lawsuit, she will be extremely wise.
6. The cost of the various procedures was never explained.
7. We will, however, be responsible for paying the contingency fee for legal counsel.
8. Don't you want to ask your client, Linda Rowan, if she has any other pertinent information regarding the case?
9. When you have all the documentation to be keyed into the computer, give it to our legal secretary, Sarah Buck.
10. JENNIFER NELSON is the plaintiff in the case. (Sentence in a legal document.) (No corrections needed.)

strained	**cannot be divided**
enough	**cannot be divided**
stormy	**cannot be divided**
disturb	**dis-turb**

Student's Name: _____

Instructor's Name: _____

Class: _____

	Date Work Submitted	Grades (Determined by Instructor)
Composition Reinforcement	_____	_____
Collaborative Research	_____	_____
Transcription Exercises	_____	_____
	_____	_____
	_____	_____
	_____	_____

Instructor's Comments Regarding Work or Suggestions for Improvement:

_____

_____

_____

_____

_____

_____

_____

_____

chapter

Bill of Sale, Complaint on Account, and Notice of Garnishment

In Chapter 13, you began your study of the legal field and typed a contingency agreement, certificate of notary, and probate court documents. This chapter will include some additional legal documents for you to transcribe.

Directions: Learn the definition for each word and how to spell it correctly. Examples of word mastery terms used during the transcription process are given below.

presents	*Definition:*	term used to identify and refer to a document itself; that is, by the facts presented
	Example:	"By these presents" is an example of a traditional phrase that appears regularly in legal instruments.
complaint	*Definition:*	a formal charge that a defendant has caused a plaintiff offense or injury
	Example:	Bailey's lawyer filed a complaint stating that Phil had taken the money.
account	*Definition:*	a record of monetary transactions
	Example:	Every bank keeps an account of the money it takes from and lends to customers.
plaintiff	*Definition:*	one who brings a legal action against a defendant
	Example:	Prospero and Caliban, Inc., was the plaintiff; and Ferdinand, the alleged trespasser on company property, was the defendant.
defendant	*Definition:*	one against whom a legal action is brought by a plaintiff
	Example:	Ferdinand will be the defendant in a lawsuit if Prospero and Caliban, Inc., take him to court for trespassing.
affidavit	*Definition:*	a written or printed declaration sworn under oath to a person with authority to administer the oath
	Example:	Because she had witnessed the accident, Elena signed an affidavit in which she stated what she had seen.
order	*Definition:*	something commanded to be done by a court of law
	Example:	The court order was that the defendant begin paying alimony.
garnishment	*Definition:*	a legal notice issued concerning the attachment of money or property of a defendant to satisfy a debt
	Example:	Aneesha's lawyer requested the court to order the garnishment of her ex-husband's salary.

garnishee	*Definition:*	the person or business whose money or property is being attached
	Example:	Daniel was the garnishee because he had refused to pay alimony.
attachment	*Definition:*	taking legal possession of a person or property
	Example:	The bank has a legal right to the attachment of Bernard's car because he failed to stay current on his payments.

Directions: Complete each sentence by filling in one of the word mastery terms. You may check your answers at the end of this chapter.

1. The attorney made sure that he had filed the _____.

2. The _____ in the case was the one who began the legal action.

3. Courtney's legal counsel advised her to sign the _____ that stated the information she knew.

4. If you do not pay your child support, a(n) _____ may be made on your salary.

5. Because a(n) _____ had been made on his vehicle, Ryan had no method of transportation.

6. Because he refused to pay child support, he became a(n) _____ so the money could be obtained.

7. Do you have a checking _____ with our local bank?

8. The plaintiff and the _____ did not even look at each other during court.

9. Because of the court _____ to do so, Michael performed several community service activities.

10. The term "By these _____" is used at the beginning of many legal documents.

Directions: Review basic grammar and punctuation rules. These rules also appear in the reference manual at the back of your text-workbook.

Rule:	When typing monetary amounts in words within legal documents, begin each word with a capital letter followed by the monetary amount written in figures.
Example:	• The defendant will pay One Thousand Five Hundred and Fifty-Five Dollars and Fifty-Five Cents ($1,555.55).

Rule:	When a word containing three or more syllables is to be divided at a one-letter syllable, key the one-letter syllable on the first line rather than the next line.
Example:	• maga-zine, not mag-azine

Rule:	When a word is divided at a point where two vowels that are pronounced separately come together, divide these vowels into separate syllables.
Example:	• situ-ation, not sit-uation or situa-tion

Directions: These examples include a review of language skills presented in the previous chapters. You may want to refer to the reference manual for a review before you begin.

Make any corrections in the following sentences. Then check your answers at the end of this chapter.

1. The plaintiff will receive One hundred forty dollars and fifty cents ($140.50). (Written in a legal document.)

2. We hope to visit Orlando, Florida on our vacation next year.

3. Therefore you must submit the information to the attorney immediately.

4. The legal office professional typed wills bills of sale and affidavits.

5. The total amount of the judgment was Three thousand five hundred dollars and forty cents ($3,500.40). (Written in a legal document.)

6. Is his law firm in Greenville South Carolina Columbia South Carolina or Charleston South Carolina.

7. Of course I hope to obtain a job as a paralegal when I graduate.

8. The amount to be awarded to the plaintiff will be three hundred dollars. (Written in a legal document.)

9. Rebecca, Susan and Lisa worked in the law firm on Main Street.

10. Nevertheless the client felt his attorney did not handle the case well.

Indicate the correct place to divide the words listed below. Then check your answers at the end of this chapter.

minimum   regular   graduation   valuable

COMPOSITION REINFORCEMENT

Directions: In the spaces provided, compose a paragraph using the word mastery terms and applying the language skills you have studied. Complete and submit your work for this assignment according to your instructor's directions.

Paragraph 1: Describe the difference between a **defendant** and a **plaintiff**.

_____

_____

_____

_____

_____

_____

_____

_____

Paragraph 2: Show how dollar amounts are written in legal documents.

_____

_____

_____

_____

_____

_____

_____

_____

Paragraph 3: Describe a **complaint**. Show proper use of word divisions.

_____

_____

_____

_____

_____

_____

Paragraph 4: Show an understanding of the word **account**. Use proper word divisions.

_____

_____

_____

_____

_____

_____

Paragraph 5: Explain **garnishee** and **garnishment**.

_____

_____

_____

_____

_____

_____

COLLABORATIVE RESEARCH

Directions: In small groups, work together to locate five recent articles from newspapers, magazines, the library, or the Internet that relate to legal ethics, legal cases, legal documents, legal terminology, or the legal profession that you did not use in previous chapters. List the source and date of each article and summarize each of the articles in the spaces provided below.

Complete and submit your work for this assignment according to your instructor's directions.

1. Source, date, and summary of article:

_____

_____

_____

_____

_____

_____

_____

2. Source, date, and summary of article:

_____

_____

_____

_____

_____

_____

_____

3. Source, date, and summary of article:

_____
_____
_____
_____
_____
_____
_____

4. Source, date, and summary of article:

_____
_____
_____
_____
_____
_____
_____

5. Source, date, and summary of article:

_____
_____
_____
_____
_____
_____
_____

TRANSCRIPTION EXERCISES

Directions: Complete all learning activities in this chapter and read all steps before beginning the transcription exercises.

1. Review the format for legal documents in the reference manual.

2. Retrieve the file from the CD for each document to be transcribed.
   - Print Document 1, a Bill of Sale that includes a Certificate of Notary, on plain paper.
   - For Document 2, open TE14-2, a Complaint on Account.
   - For Document 3, open TE14-3, an Affidavit, Court Order, and Notice of Garnishment.

3. For Documents 2 and 3, remember to use the Save As feature and an appropriate filename.

4. In Documents 2 and 3, you will be required to key the variable information into the underlined spaces provided in the file. Remove the underlines after you have supplied the information. *Be sure to read the entire document after you have supplied the information dictated so you are familiar with the content of the documents.*

5. Transcribe all the legal documents on the CD in acceptable form using the current date unless another date is given.

6. Proofread, spell-check, and submit all documents to your instructor for approval.

CHAPTER *Checkpoints*

Upon completion of the various learning activities in this chapter, you should be able to meet the objectives listed at the beginning of this chapter. If you feel you cannot answer "yes" to all of the statements listed below, consult your instructor.

Directions: *Place a check mark (✓) in the box for all that apply.*

☐ I can define and use the word mastery terms presented in this chapter.

☐ I can apply the number and word division rules presented in this chapter and punctuation and grammar rules presented in earlier chapters and in the reference manual.

☐ I can compose paragraphs in acceptable form utilizing the word mastery terms and language skills presented in this chapter.

☐ I can use my researching, writing, and communication skills correctly.

☐ I can transcribe legal documents in acceptable form.

Answers to Word Mastery Self-Check

1. The attorney made sure that he had filed the **complaint**.
2. The **plaintiff** in the case was the one who began the legal action.
3. Courtney's legal counsel advised her to sign the **affidavit** that stated the information she knew.
4. If you do not pay your child support, a **garnishment** may be made on your salary.
5. Because an **attachment** had been made on his vehicle, Ryan had no method of transportation.
6. Because he refused to pay child support, he became a **garnishee** so the money could be obtained.
7. Do you have a checking **account** with our local bank?
8. The plaintiff and the **defendant** did not even look at each other during court.
9. Because of the court **order** to do so, Michael performed several community service activities.
10. The term "By these **presents**" is used at the beginning of many legal documents.

Answers to Language Skills Self-Check

1. The plaintiff will receive One Hundred Forty Dollars and Fifty Cents ($140.50). (Written in a legal document.)
2. We hope to visit Orlando, Florida, on our vacation next year.
3. Therefore, you must submit the information to the attorney immediately.
4. The legal office professional typed wills, bills of sale, and affidavits.
5. The total amount of the judgment was Three Thousand Five Hundred Dollars and Forty Cents ($3,500.40). (Written in a legal document.)
6. Is his law firm in Greenville, South Carolina; Columbia, South Carolina; or Charleston, South Carolina?
7. Of course, I hope to obtain a job as a paralegal when I graduate.
8. The amount to be awarded to the plaintiff will be Three Hundred Dollars ($300.00). (Written in a legal document.)
9. Rebecca, Susan, and Lisa worked in the law firm on Main Street.
10. Nevertheless, the client felt his attorney did not handle the case well.

minimum	**mini-mum**
regular	**regu-lar**
graduation	**gradu-ation**
valuable	**valu-able**

Student's Name: _____

Instructor's Name: _____

Class: _____

	Date Work Submitted	Grades (Determined by Instructor)
Composition Reinforcement	_____	_____
Collaborative Research	_____	_____
Transcription Exercises	_____	_____
	_____	_____
	_____	_____

Instructor's Comments Regarding Work or Suggestions for Improvement:

_____

_____

_____

_____

_____

_____

_____

_____

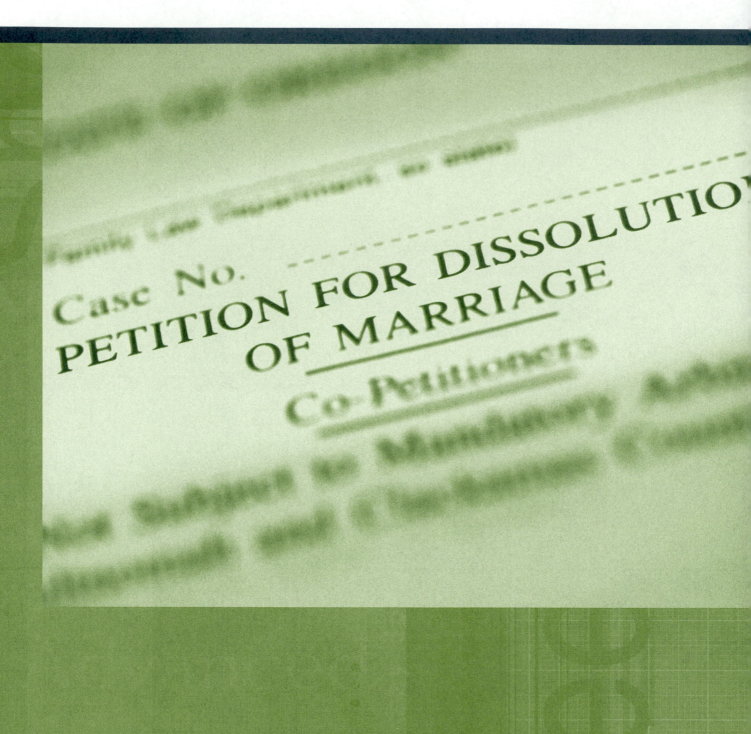

Petition for Dissolution of Marriage and Billing Statements

B ill of Sale, Complaint on Account, Affidavit, Order and Notice of Garnishment Forms were presented in Chapter 14. Chapter 15 will focus on other documents processed in legal offices.

Directions: Learn the definition for each word and how to spell it correctly. Examples of word mastery terms used during the transcription process are given below.

petition

Definition: a written application to the court for action on a legal matter

Example: Wes and Angie's attorney filed a petition for them to adopt a baby.

dissolution

Definition: the separation or breaking of a legal bond or tie

Example: Dion and Jane were granted a dissolution of their marriage.

filing

Definition: placing papers with the clerk of a court

Example: Joanne is filing to start her business under the name "Stylus, Inc.," but she must wait to see if the name is already being used.

petitioners

Definition: the people who file a legal request

Example: The petitioners filed a lawsuit in probate court.

residents

Definition: those who live in a certain place

Example: Janis and Hunter have been residents of this apartment building for many years.

issue

Definition: offspring; children

Example: When someone dies without issue, that person will often leave his or her estate to relatives or close friends.

amendments

Definition: corrections or changes

Example: When she reread her essay, Myrna made amendments to one of her reference notes.

decree

Definition: an order or a decision issued by a legal authority

Example: The judge's decree stated that Rita and Raoul's marriage was officially dissolved.

statement	*Definition:*	a report of money owed for services performed
	Example:	Bridget prepared the client's statement for last month.
retainer	*Definition:*	the fee paid to an attorney for hiring the attorney on an as-needed basis
	Example:	Our company has an attorney on retainer who charges for every phone call we make to her.

WORD MASTERY *Self-Check*

Directions: Complete each sentence by filling in one of the word mastery terms. You may check your answers at the end of this chapter.

1. Although they had been partners for years, the attorneys filed a(n) _____ of that partnership.

2. The _____ of the house were not home.

3. Several _____ had to be made to the proposal before it was presented to the Board of Directors.

4. Jackson never received his monthly _____ from the company.

5. Because he was on _____ with the client, he rescheduled his previous commitment to talk with the client.

6. The young couple plan on _____ for divorce within the next week.

7. Thelma and Louise were the _____ who filed the lawsuit against their employers.

8. Gabriella made a(n) _____ to the court regarding the changing of her name.

9. The judge's _____ will be the final decision regarding the case.

10. Because Aunt Tilley died without _____, she left her entire estate to her niece, Katie.

Directions: Review basic grammar and punctuation rules. These rules also appear in the reference manual.

Rule:	Use the abbreviation Re: in legal letters to represent regarding or subject.
Example:	• Re: Dissolution of Marriage (subject line within a legal letter)
Rule:	If there are double consonants in a base word, divide the word between the double consonants.
Example:	• recom-mend
Rule:	When a suffix is added to a word that ends in double letters, divide the word after the double letters if there is a syllable break between the double letters and the suffix.
Examples:	• fill-ing
	• kissed (cannot be divided even though the word ends in double letters before the suffix is added to the word because this is a one-syllable word)
Rule:	If a final consonant is doubled when a suffix is added to a word, divide the word between the double letters.
Example:	• refer-ring

LANGUAGE SKILLS *Self-Check*

Directions: These examples include a review of language skills presented in the previous chapters. You may want to refer to the reference manual for a review before you begin.

Make any corrections in the following sentences. Then check your answers at the end of this chapter.

1. The intelligent young attorney approached the judges bench.

2. We need to decide our law firms long range goals.

3. She typed all of the legal documents for the day and she proceeded to file all of the material that needed to be filed.

4. Several attorneys desks needed to be moved into the next office.

5. We wanted the well known author to sign his book for us.

6. Because an attractive well dressed man was sitting behind the desk in the law office the clients assumed he was their attorney.

7. The paralegals were researching information the attorneys needed and they discovered some interesting facts.

8. Don't you want to contact a well educated attorney to handle the case for you.

9. The legal assistants notes were nowhere to be found, even though she looked in several locations.

10. Since you have taken several legal and clerical courses finding a well paying rewarding position should not be difficult.

Indicate the correct place to divide the words listed below. Then check your answers at the end of this chapter.

slipping   embarrass   callers   occurred

COMPOSITION REINFORCEMENT

Directions: In the spaces provided, compose a paragraph using the word mastery terms and applying the language skills you have studied. Complete and submit your work for this assignment according to your instructor's directions.

Paragraph 1: Explain how the terms **petition** and **petitioners** are related.

_____

_____

_____

_____

_____

_____

_____

Paragraph 2: Explain the term **dissolution**. Use proper syllable divisions.

_____

_____

_____

_____

_____

_____

_____

_____

Paragraph 3: Show an understanding of the word **amendments**.

_____

_____

_____

_____

_____

_____

Paragraph 4: Who are **residents**? Are you a resident?

_____

_____

_____

_____

_____

_____

_____

Paragraph 5: Explain the kind of statement you might receive from an attorney's office.

_____

_____

_____

_____

_____

_____

_____

COLLABORATIVE RESEARCH

Directions: In small groups, work together to locate five recent articles from newspapers, magazines, the library, or the Internet that relate to legal ethics, legal cases, legal documents, legal terminology, or the legal profession that you did not use in previous chapters. List the source and date of each article and summarize each of the articles in the spaces provided below.

Complete and submit your work for this assignment according to your instructor's directions.

1. Source, date, and summary of article:

_____

_____

_____

_____

_____

_____

_____

2. Source, date, and summary of article:

_____

_____

_____

_____

_____

_____

_____

3. Source, date, and summary of article:

_____

_____

_____

_____

_____

_____

4. Source, date, and summary of article:

_____

_____

_____

_____

_____

_____

5. Source, date, and summary of article:

_____

_____

_____

_____

_____

_____

TRANSCRIPTION EXERCISES

Directions: Complete all learning activities in this chapter and read all steps before beginning the transcription exercises.

1. Review the format for legal documents in the reference manual.

2. Retrieve the file from the student CD for each document to be transcribed.
   - For Document 1, open TE15-1, letterhead for the Simonson law firm.
   - Print Document 2, Petition for Dissolution of Marriage, on plain paper.
   - For Document 3, open TE15-3, Billing Statement.

3. For Documents 2 and 3, use the Save As feature and an appropriate filename.

4. Use the block style letter with mixed punctuation for Document 1. In Document 3 you will be required to key the variable information into the underlined spaces provided in the file. Remove the underlines after you have supplied the information. *Be sure to read the entire document after you have supplied the information dictated so you are familiar with the content of the document.*

5. Transcribe all the legal documents on the student CD in acceptable form using the current date unless another date is given.

6. Proofread, spell-check, and submit all documents to your instructor for approval.

CHAPTER *Checkpoints*

Upon completion of the various learning activities in this chapter, you should be able to meet the objectives listed at the beginning of this chapter. If you feel you cannot answer "yes" to all of the statements listed below, consult your instructor.

Directions: *Place a check mark (✔) in the box for all that apply.*

☐ I can define and use the word mastery terms presented in this chapter.

☐ I can apply the abbreviation and word division rules presented in this chapter and punctuation and grammar rules presented in earlier chapters and in the reference manual.

☐ I can compose paragraphs in acceptable form utilizing the word mastery terms and language skills presented in this chapter.

☐ I can use my researching, writing, and communication skills correctly.

☐ I can transcribe legal documents in acceptable form.

Answers to Word Mastery Self-Check

1. Although they had been partners for years, the attorneys filed a **dissolution** of that partnership.
2. The **residents** of the house were not home.
3. Several **amendments** had to be made to the proposal before it was presented to the Board of Directors.
4. Jackson never received his monthly **statement** from the company.
5. Because he was on **retainer** with the client, he rescheduled his previous commitment to talk with the client.
6. The young couple plan on **filing** for divorce within the next week.
7. Thelma and Louise were the **petitioners** who filed the lawsuit against their employers.
8. Gabriella made a **petition** to the court regarding the changing of her name.
9. The judge's **decree** will be the final decision regarding the case.
10. Because Aunt Tilley died without **issue**, she left her entire estate to her niece, Katie.

Answers to Language Skills Self-Check

1. The intelligent, young attorney approached the judge's bench.
2. We need to decide our law firm's long-range goals.
3. She typed all of the legal documents for the day, and she proceeded to file all of the material that needed to be filed.
4. Several attorneys' desks needed to be moved into the next office.
5. We wanted the well-known author to sign his book for us.
6. Because an attractive, well-dressed man was sitting behind the desk in the law office, the clients assumed he was their attorney.
7. The paralegals were researching information the attorneys needed, and they discovered some interesting facts.
8. Don't you want to contact a well-educated attorney to handle the case for you?
9. The legal assistant's notes were nowhere to be found, even though she looked in several locations.
10. Since you have taken several legal and clerical courses, finding a well-paying, rewarding position should not be difficult.

slipping	**slip-ping**
embarrass	**embar-rass**
callers	**call-ers**
occurred	**oc-curred (cannot be divided occur-red because there is not a syllable at this point)**

Student's Name: _____

Instructor's Name: _____

Class: _____

	Date Work Submitted	Grades (Determined by Instructor)
Composition Reinforcement	_____	_____
Collaborative Research	_____	_____
Transcription Exercises	_____	_____
	_____	_____
	_____	_____

Instructor's Comments Regarding Work or Suggestions for Improvement:

_____

_____

_____

_____

_____

_____

_____

_____

chapter

16

Estate and Tax Matters

This chapter will give you experience in keying correspondence as well as doing a form letter in which you insert the variable information.

Directions: Learn the definition for each word and how to spell it correctly. Examples of word mastery terms used during the transcription process are given below.

tax	*Definition:*	payment required from a person, business, or property owner to support and maintain a government
	Example:	My parents must pay a property tax on the land they own.
status	*Definition:*	the condition, state, or rank of someone or something
	Example:	Mike's status among his colleagues was elevated when they learned that he had been promoted.
citizen	*Definition:*	a person owing loyalty to and entitled to the protection of a government, either by birthright or by having been given such a right by that government
	Example:	Raymond, who was born in Bathurst, is a Gambian citizen.
fiscal	*Definition:*	having to do with finances, especially those of a government
	Example:	The United States' fiscal policies changed dramatically during the Great Depression of the 1930s.
evasion	*Definition:*	the act of avoiding or eluding
	Example:	Because he did not know the answer to the instructor's question, the student talked in generalities in an attempt at evasion.
compensation	*Definition:*	payment
	Example:	In return for compensation, Lawrence is to work efficiently 40 hours each week.
substantiate	*Definition:*	to verify or establish something as true
	Example:	The attorney learned that her client had not been honest and could not substantiate what she had claimed.
executor	*Definition:*	one named by the maker of a will to fulfill the terms of the will after the maker's death
	Example:	Kim received her parents' home and property through her Uncle Brad, who had been named executor of the estate.

estate	*Definition:*	any kind of property that an individual owns and can dispose of in a will
	Example:	The millionaire's estate was divided equally among his children.
rights	*Definition:*	proper and lawful claim to or interest in something
	Example:	Maria just sold the rights to her first song to a record company.
carry-ons	*Definition:*	series of books continuing the story of the same character
	Example:	After reading the first book, I was anxious to read the other carry-ons that the author had written about the heroine.
pastiches	*Definition:*	pieces of literary, artistic, musical, or architectural work that imitate the style of previous work
	Example:	The author's pastiches were best-sellers because readers had enjoyed his previous books.
contract	*Definition:*	a legally binding, formal agreement between two or more parties
	Example:	Before her first book was published, Benedicta signed a contract in which she agreed to terms of the sale, distribution of the books, and payment of royalties.

Directions: Complete each sentence by filling in one of the word mastery terms. You may check your answers at the end of this chapter.

1. Have you paid the property _____ on the car you bought?

2. Although Els was born in Holland, she is now a(n) _____ of the United States.

3. Will I receive the _____ we agreed upon when I signed my contract?

4. Trevor was the _____ of his wife's estate.

5. You will have to relinquish all _____ to the property when you sell it to someone else.

6. When they formed their partnership, each one signed a(n) _____ listing the terms of their agreement.

7. Roxanne's attorney suggested she make plans regarding her _____ to ensure that her assets would be distributed as she wanted when she died.

8. You will need to _____ your whereabouts during the time of the murder.

9. The _____ year of many companies does not correspond with the calendar year.

10. Tax _____ may occur; however, one may eventually be caught and will face stern penalties for doing this.

Directions: Review basic grammar and punctuation rules. These rules also appear in the reference manual at the back of your text-workbook.

Rule: Divide a compound word between the elements of the compound word.

Example: • eye-witness not eyewit-ness

Rule: Divide hyphenated words only at the hyphen.

Example: • self-confident not self-confi-dent

Rule: When dividing a date, divide between the day of the month and the year. A hyphen is not used in this division.

Example: • August 13,
2001

not

August
13, 2001

Rule: When dividing a name, divide between the middle initial and the surname. If no middle initial is given, divide between the given name and surname. Do not separate titles from the given name or from the surname if the given name is not given. Hyphens are not used in this division.

Examples: • Mary E.   Mrs. Mary   Dr. Gonzales
Cohen   Cohen

not   *not*   *not*

Mary   Mrs.   Dr.
E. Cohen   Mary Cohen   Gonzales

Rule: If it is necessary to separate an address within a sentence, keep together the number and street name and the state and ZIP code. You may separate an address between the street name and city name or the city name and the state name. Hyphens are not used in this division.

Example: • 123 Rowan Street
Nashville, TN 37203-6109

not

123
Rowan Street
Nashville,
TN 37203-6109

Directions: These examples include a review of language skills presented in the previous chapters. You may want to refer to the reference manual in the back of this text-workbook for a review before you begin.

Make any corrections in the following sentences. Then check your answers at the end of this chapter.

1. Be sure to consult your attorney Roddy before you go to court.

2. In August we hope our family can all join us for our family vacation.

3. The paraprofessionals and office staff were all at lunch therefore no one could assist the attorney with the paperwork for the case.

4. Some students in the class indicated they wanted to pursue a career in the legal field other students stated they preferred the medical field.

5. The stress of the day of course took its toll on everyone in the office but they all knew they had to complete the report make copies and collate the material before the meeting.

6. Of course everyone wants to do his/her best but this does not mean everything will be done to perfection.

7. Her daughter Karen decided to pursue a paralegal career, her daughter Gracie decided to pursue a legal secretary career.

8. In the afternoon the attorney preferred to have no appointments scheduled after 4 p.m.

9. At the very last moment we realized we had not scheduled the conference room for the meeting.

10. We cannot afford to hire any more full time staff however we can hire some part time employees temporarily.

Indicate the correct place to divide the words listed below. Then check your answers at the end of this chapter.

checkbook   self-fulfilled   January 31, 2002   Mr. Juan Diego

COMPOSITION REINFORCEMENT

Directions: In the spaces provided, compose five paragraphs using the word mastery terms and applying the language skills you have studied. Complete and submit your work for this assignment according to your instructor's directions.

Paragraph 1: What are your responsibilities and rights as a citizen of the United States?

_____

_____

_____

_____

_____

_____

_____

_____

Paragraph 2: Describe a time you may have practiced evasion of some kind.

_____

_____

_____

_____

_____

_____

_____

_____

Paragraph 3: Describe a time you have received compensation for something you have done.

_____

_____

_____

_____

_____

_____

Paragraph 4: Send a mock invitation to someone and show an understanding of date, name, and address division.

_____

_____

_____

_____

_____

_____

Paragraph 5: How does your status compare to that of your instructor?

_____

_____

_____

_____

_____

_____

COLLABORATIVE RESEARCH

Directions: In small groups, work together to locate five recent articles from newspapers, magazines, the library, or the Internet that relate to legal ethics, legal cases, legal documents, legal terminology, or the legal profession that you did not use in previous chapters. List the source and date of each article and summarize each of the articles in the spaces provided below.

Complete and submit your work for this assignment according to your instructor's directions.

1. Source, date, and summary of article:

_____

_____

_____

_____

_____

_____

2. Source, date, and summary of article:

_____

_____

_____

_____

_____

_____

3. Source, date, and summary of article:

_____

_____

_____

_____

_____

_____

4. Source, date, and summary of article:

_____

_____

_____

_____

_____

_____

_____

5. Source, date, and summary of article:

_____

_____

_____

_____

_____

_____

_____

Directions: Complete all learning activities in this chapter and read all steps before beginning the transcription exercises.

1. Review the format for legal documents in the reference manual.

2. Retrieve the file from the student CD for each document to be transcribed.
   - For Document 1, open TE16-1, letterhead for Simonson, Kodaly, Blum & Brathwaite.
   - For Document 2, open TE16-2, a form letter for Simonson, Kodaly, Blum & Brathwaite.
   - For Document 3, open TE16-3, a form letter for Simonson, Kodaly, Blum & Brathwaite.

3. Remember to use the Save As feature and the name of the individual to whom the document was addressed as the filename.

4. Use the block style letter with mixed punctuation for Document 1. In Documents 2 and 3 you will be required to key the variable information in the underlined spaces provided in the file. *Be sure to read the entire document after you have supplied the information dictated so you are familiar with the content of the documents.*

5. Transcribe all the legal documents on the CD in acceptable form using the current date unless another date is given.

6. Proofread, spell-check, and submit all documents to your instructor for approval.

CHAPTER *Checkpoints*

Upon completion of the various learning activities in this chapter, you should be able to meet the objectives listed at the beginning of this chapter. If you feel you cannot answer "yes" to all of the statements listed below, consult your instructor.

Directions: *Place a check mark (✔) in the box for all that apply.*

☐ I can define and use the word mastery terms presented in this chapter.

☐ I can apply the word division rules presented in this chapter and punctuation and grammar rules presented in earlier chapters and in the reference manual.

☐ I can compose paragraphs in acceptable form utilizing the word mastery terms and language skills presented in this chapter.

☐ I can use my researching, writing, and communication skills correctly.

☐ I can transcribe legal documents in acceptable form.

ANSWER KEY FOR *Self-Checks*

Answers to Word Mastery Self-Check

1. Have you paid the property **tax** on the car you bought?
2. Although Els was born in Holland, she is now a **citizen** of the United States.
3. Will I receive the **compensation** we agreed upon when I signed my contract?
4. Trevor was the **executor** of his wife's estate.
5. You will have to relinquish all **rights** to the property when you sell it to someone else.
6. When they formed their partnership, each one signed a **contract** listing the terms of their agreement.
7. Roxanne's attorney suggested she make plans regarding her **estate** to ensure that her assets would be distributed as she wanted when she died.
8. You will need to **substantiate** your whereabouts during the time of the murder.
9. The **fiscal** year of many companies does not correspond with the calendar year.
10. Tax **evasion** may occur; however, one may eventually be caught and will face stern penalties for doing this.

Answers to Language Skills Self-Check

1. Be sure to consult your attorney, Roddy, before you go to court.
2. In August we hope our family can all join us for our family vacation. (No corrections needed.)
3. The paraprofessionals and office staff were all at lunch; therefore, no one could assist the attorney with the paperwork for the case.
4. Some students in the class indicated they wanted to pursue a career in the legal field; other students stated they preferred the medical field.
5. The stress of the day, of course, took its toll on everyone in the office; but they all knew they had to complete the report, make copies, and collate the material before the meeting.
6. Of course, everyone wants to do his/her best; but this does not mean everything will be done to perfection.
7. Her daughter, Karen, decided to pursue a paralegal career; her daughter, Gracie, decided to pursue a legal secretary career.
8. In the afternoon the attorney preferred to have no appointments scheduled after 4 p.m. (No corrections needed.)
9. At the very last moment, we realized we had not scheduled the conference room for the meeting.
10. We cannot afford to hire any more full-time staff; however, we can hire some part-time employees temporarily.

checkbook	**check-book**	January 31, 2002	**January 31, 2002**
self-fulfilled	**self-fulfilled**		
		Mr. Juan Diego	**Mr. Juan Diego**

EVALUATION FORM

Student's Name: _____

Instructor's Name: _____

Class: _____

	Date Work Submitted	Grades (Determined by Instructor)
Composition Reinforcement	_____	_____
Collaborative Research	_____	_____
Transcription Exercises	_____	_____
	_____	_____
	_____	_____
	_____	_____

Instructor's Comments Regarding Work or Suggestions for Improvement:

_____

_____

_____

_____

_____

_____

_____

_____

chapter

Consultation Letter, Medical Memorandum, and Mammogram Report

The medical field provides one of the most exciting opportunities for employment in the 2000s. Careers await trained personnel in private doctors' offices, hospitals, clinics, insurance companies, nursing homes, and outpatient facilities. In all areas of the United States, the medical field is expanding. As people live longer, the demand for medical services will continue to grow.

The medical field uses medical transcription extensively. Medical transcriptionists and medical office personnel are needed in all types of medical facilities. Because some medical terms and medicines are similar, a person who transcribes medical documents must be extremely accurate. Courses in medical terminology, anatomy, and biology are essential for someone who wants to consider medical transcription as a career.

LEARNING OBJECTIVES

After completing all the learning activities in this chapter, you will be able to:

Define and use the word mastery terms presented in this chapter correctly.

Apply the medical prefixes and suffixes presented in this chapter.

Compose paragraphs in acceptable form utilizing the word mastery terms and language skills presented in this chapter.

Utilize your researching, writing, and communication skills correctly in a collaborative research activity.

Transcribe medical documents in acceptable form.

Directions: Learn the definition for each word and how to spell it correctly. Examples of word mastery terms used during the transcription process are given below.

| **cardiovascular** | *Definition:* | involving the heart and the blood vessels |
| | *Example:* | Regular exercise contributes to the health of the cardiovascular system. |

| **arteriogram** | *Definition:* | an x-ray of an artery |
| | *Example:* | An arteriogram is performed when a cardiologist suspects a heart blockage. |

| **infarction** | *Definition:* | the formation of a portion of dying or dead tissue |
| | *Example:* | The formation of a blood clot is a common cause of infarction. |

| **mammogram** | *Definition:* | an x-ray of the breast |
| | *Example:* | A regular mammogram is recommended for women as an early detection of breast cancer. |

| **calcifications** | *Definition:* | deposits of calcium salts in body tissue |
| | *Example:* | Calcifications in soft tissue are abnormal. |

| **intraductal** | *Definition:* | within a duct |
| | *Example:* | The dye was injected into the body by an intraductal method. |

| **carcinoma** | *Definition:* | a malignant new growth made up of cells tending to spread to surrounding tissues; a form of cancer |
| | *Example:* | Carcinoma refers to a cancerous tumor. |

| **biopsy** | *Definition:* | removal and examination of a small amount of tissue from the body |
| | *Example:* | A biopsy is often performed when a suspicious lump is found in the breast. |

| **benign** | *Definition:* | not malignant; not cancerous |
| | *Example:* | He was relieved that the tumor was benign. |

axillary

Definition: pertaining to the armpit

Example: The axillary area is often affected as the result of a mastectomy.

asymmetrical

Definition: dissimilarity in appearance of body parts that should appear as the same size and shape

Example: The right eye was slanted more than the left, causing an asymmetrical appearance.

Directions: Complete each sentence by filling in one of the word mastery terms. You may check your answers at the end of this chapter.

1. Sylvia always has her _____ done on a yearly basis.

2. When the doctors examined the x-rays more closely, they decided that the areas of concern were merely _____.

3. After the procedure was performed, the doctors could tell more from the _____ taken from her left breast.

4. Ralph hoped his tumor was _____ and not malignant.

5. Sometimes tissue from the _____ area must be removed if breast cancer has been found.

6. The _____ appearance of his ears made him look quite unusual.

7. Since he did not exercise and watch what he ate, it is no surprise that he had _____ disease at an early age.

8. _____ is a form of cancer.

9. If your physician suspects some heart blockage, he may perform a(n) _____.

10. A(n) _____ can occur if you have a blood clot.

Directions: Knowing various prefixes and suffixes used within the medical fields will help you become more familiar with the meanings of medical terms. In the language skills sections of this chapter and Chapters 18 through 20, you will be introduced to various prefixes and suffixes. Some of these prefixes and suffixes are used in the word mastery terms you are studying within the chapter. Learn each prefix or suffix and its meaning.

Prefix or Suffix	Meaning
ambi-	on both sides
anti-	against
arterio-	artery
auto-	self
bi-	two
carcino-	carcinoma
cardio-	heart
-gram	record
intra-	within
mammo-	breast

Directions: These examples include a review of language skills presented in the previous chapters. You may want to refer to the reference manual for a review before you begin.

Make any corrections in the following sentences. Then check your answers at the end of this chapter.

1. Our medical office will now be located at 23 East 5th Avenue.

2. We found $.50 under the sofa as we were cleaning the physician's office.

3. The medical secretary informed the physician he had eleven more patients in the waiting room to see him.

4. After studying for the test, the student felt she still did not know fifty percent of the medical prefixes and suffixes.

5. Manuel Martinez had an appointment on the 5 of May to see his physician.

6. Your doctor's appointment was scheduled for June 5.

7. There is a eighty percent chance he will recover from the accident.

8. Please visit our new location at 1 West 10th Avenue.

9. Your bill for the office visit today will be $95.00.

10. Of the 10 nurses that were hired last year, 2 decided to resign.

Fill in the prefixes or suffixes for the meanings listed below.

record   _____

breast   _____

heart   _____

artery   _____

within   _____

COMPOSITION REINFORCEMENT

Directions: In the spaces provided, compose five paragraphs using the word mastery terms and applying the language skills you have studied. Complete and submit your work for this assignment according to your instructor's directions.

Paragraph 1: How might the words **cardiovascular** and **arteriogram** be related?

_____

_____

_____

_____

_____

_____

_____

Paragraph 2: Having a yearly mammogram is important. Why?

_____

_____

_____

_____

_____

_____

_____

Paragraph 3: Set up a mock doctor's appointment for someone, showing an understanding of use of dates, times, and addresses.

_____

_____

_____

_____

_____

_____

Paragraph 4: Compare the terms **carcinoma** and **benign**.

_____

_____

_____

_____

_____

_____

Paragraph 5: Why would it be important to know medical prefixes and suffixes?

_____

_____

_____

_____

_____

_____

_____

COLLABORATIVE RESEARCH

Directions: In small groups, work together to answer each numbered item. You may find answers by researching the Internet, newspaper, and library; or you may want to talk with individuals who are actually employed in this field.

When searching the Internet, you may want to go to **http://www. bls.gov,** click on Publications and Research Papers, click on Occupational Outlook Handbook, and click on the Index to the Handbook for the letter that begins with the word of the field. You also may find information by searching under the name of the field/industry mentioned in the chapter followed by the words *career* or *training. Example: medical career* or *medical training.*

Complete and submit your work for this assignment according to your instructor's directions.

1. Research the employment opportunities for office workers and list the advantages and/or disadvantages of employment in the medical field.

_____

_____

_____

_____

_____

_____

_____

2. List the skills or characteristics that are necessary to work in this field.

_____

_____

_____

_____

_____

_____

_____

3. List the various job titles or positions in this field.

_____

_____

_____

_____

_____

_____

4. List the salary ranges for positions in this field.

_____

_____

_____

_____

_____

_____

5. List any additional information you learned during your research.

_____

_____

_____

_____

_____

_____

Directions: Complete all learning activities in this chapter and read all steps before beginning the transcription exercises.

1. Review the format for block letters, memorandums, and medical documents in the reference manual.

2. Retrieve the file from the student CD for each document to be transcribed.
   - For Document 1, open TE17-1, the letterhead for Vanessa T. Melvin, M.D.
   - Print the memorandum in Document 2 on plain paper.
   - For Document 3, open TE17-3, a Mammogram Report.

3. For Documents 1 and 3, remember to use the Save As feature and an appropriate filename.

4. Use the block style letter with mixed punctuation for Document 1. Use the standard interoffice memorandum style for Document 2. Insert the information for Document 3 that is dictated on the tape. *Be sure to read the entire document after you have supplied the information dictated so you are familiar with the content of the document.*

5. Transcribe all the medical documents from the student CD in acceptable form using the current date unless another date is given.

6. Proofread, spell-check, and submit all documents to your instructor for approval.

CHAPTER *Checkpoints*

Upon completion of the various learning activities in this chapter, you should be able to meet the objectives listed at the beginning of this chapter. If you feel you cannot answer "yes" to all of the statements listed below, consult your instructor.

Directions: *Place a check mark (✓) in the box for all that apply.*

☐ I can define and use the word mastery terms presented in this chapter.

☐ I can apply the prefixes and suffixes presented in this chapter.

☐ I can compose paragraphs in acceptable form utilizing the word mastery terms and language skills presented in this chapter.

☐ I can use my researching, writing, and communication skills correctly.

☐ I can transcribe medical documents in acceptable form.

Answers to Word Mastery Self-Check

1. Sylvia always has her **mammogram** done on a yearly basis.
2. When the doctors examined the x-rays more closely, they decided that the areas of concern were merely **calcifications**.
3. After the procedure was performed, the doctors could tell more from the **biopsy** taken from her left breast.
4. Ralph hoped his tumor was **benign** and not malignant.
5. Sometimes tissue from the **axillary** area must be removed if breast cancer has been found.
6. The **asymmetrical** appearance of his ears made him look quite unusual.
7. Since he did not exercise and watch what he ate, it is no surprise that he had **cardiovascular** disease at an early age.
8. **Carcinoma** is a form of cancer.
9. If your physician suspects some heart blockage, he may perform an **arteriogram**.
10. An **infarction** can occur if you have a blood clot.

Answers to Language Skills Self-Check

1. Our medical office will now be located at 23 East Fifth Avenue.
2. We found 50 cents under the sofa as we were cleaning the physician's office.
3. The medical secretary informed the physician he had 11 more patients in the waiting room to see him.
4. After studying for the test, the student felt she still did not know 50 percent of the medical prefixes and suffixes.
5. Manuel Martinez had an appointment on the 5th of May to see his physician.
6. Your doctor's appointment was scheduled for June 5. (No corrections needed.)
7. There is an 80 percent chance he will recover from the accident.
8. Please visit our new location at One West Tenth Avenue.
9. Your bill for the office visit today will be $95.
10. Of the ten nurses that were hired last year, two decided to resign.

record	**-gram**
breast	**mammo-**
heart	**cardio-**
artery	**arterio-**
within	**intra-**

Student's Name: _____

Instructor's Name: _____

Class: _____

	Date Work Submitted	Grades (Determined by Instructor)
Composition Reinforcement	_____	_____
Collaborative Research	_____	_____
Transcription Exercises	_____	_____
	_____	_____
	_____	_____

Instructor's Comments Regarding Work or Suggestions for Improvement:

_____

_____

_____

_____

_____

_____

_____

_____

_____

chapter

Report of Radiologist and Relocation Announcement

*P*atients today may choose to have routine x-rays done at an outpatient radiology facility as a less costly alternative to hospital admission and testing. Radiology offices provide another opportunity for the medical transcriptionist. Results from procedures involving anteroposterior (AP) x-ray, nuclear medicine, low-dose mammography, ultrasound, Computerized tomography (CT), and magnetic resonance imaging (MRI) must be transcribed into a variety of reports.

LEARNING OBJECTIVES

After completing all the learning activities in this chapter, you will be able to:

Define and use the word mastery terms presented in this chapter correctly.

Apply the medical prefixes and suffixes presented in this chapter.

Compose paragraphs in acceptable form utilizing the word mastery terms and language skills presented in this chapter.

Utilize your researching, writing, and communication skills correctly in a collaborative research activity.

Transcribe medical documents in acceptable form.

Directions: Learn the definition for each word and how to spell it correctly. Examples of word mastery terms used during the transcription process are given below.

demineralization	*Definition:*	excessive elimination of mineral or organic salts from the tissues of the body
	Example:	Digesting one thousand milligrams of calcium per day can help prevent demineralization of the bones.
degenerative	*Definition:*	deteriorating
	Example:	Degenerative arthritis can be very painful.
arthritic	*Definition:*	pertaining to the inflammation of a joint
	Example:	The Arthritis Foundation supports research for arthritis that helps sufferers of arthritic pain lead productive lives.
spurring	*Definition:*	the projection of a growth that extends from the bone
	Example:	Spinal arthritic spurring can cause a patient great discomfort.
spondylolisthesis	*Definition:*	forward displacement of a vertebra over a lower portion of the spine due to an inborn defect or fracture
	Example:	For temporary relief of spondylolisthesis, the patient saw the chiropractor for spinal manipulation.
apophyseal	*Definition:*	pertaining to any outgrowth or swelling, especially a bony outgrowth that has never been entirely separated from the bone of which it forms a part
	Example:	The apophyseal joints were best demonstrated on the lumbar views.
levoscoliosis	*Definition:*	a left-sided abnormal curving of the spinal column
	Example:	Levoscoliosis can cause neck and back pain.
acute	*Definition:*	sudden; sharp; severe
	Example:	An acute illness is serious but only lasts for a short period of time.

aorta	*Definition:*	the largest artery in the body, arising from the left ventricle; the main trunk from which the systemic arterial system proceeds.
	Example:	The aorta is the largest artery in the body.
Magnetic Resonance Imaging (MRI)	*Definition:*	an imaging technique used to diagnose cancer and other tumors and masses of the soft tissues
	Example:	A patient must lie motionless in the center of a tube during the magnetic resonance imaging process.

Directions: Complete each sentence by filling in one of the word mastery terms. You may check your answers at the end of this chapter.

1. Her doctor thought the pain was from _____ arthritis.

2. Those who suffer from _____ can often find relief from pain by visiting a chiropractor for adjustment of the spine.

3. Many children are checked for _____ when they visit their pediatricians for a yearly physical.

4. Her _____ headache even caused her to have vision problems.

5. Although she was scared to have the _____ _____ _____ performed, she discovered there was no pain involved.

6. _____ pain occurs in many senior adults as the body ages.

7. Arthritic _____ causes severe pain.

8. The doctor prescribed calcium to his patient to help prevent _____ of her bones.

9. The _____ is an artery in the heart.

10. When the doctor looked at the x-rays, he could see the _____ joints.

Directions: Knowing various prefixes and suffixes used within the medical fields will help you become more familiar with the meanings of medical terms. Some of the prefixes and suffixes listed below are used in the word mastery terms you are studying within the chapter. Learn each prefix or suffix and its meaning.

Prefix or Suffix	Meaning
-cyte	cell
de-	lack of
di-	two, twice
-ectomy	removal
hemi-	half
hemato-	blood
inter-	between
macro-	large
micro-	small
neo-	new

Directions: These examples include a review of language skills presented in the previous chapters. You may want to refer to the reference manual for a review before you begin.

Make any corrections in the following sentences. Then check your answers at the end of this chapter.

1. The interns will need to attend the orientation meeting at 3 o'clock.

2. Check the patient's blood pressure, temperature, and other vital signs—these were the procedures she was to follow.

3. If and only if you must leave the class, be sure you ask someone to take notes for you.

4. This is an emergency.

5. The following students will be graduating from the program Tomas Medina, Margarita Flores, and Oki Beppu.

6. Anatomy pathology and pharmacology these courses need to be taken before you proceed with the medical transcription course.

7. I cannot stress that you follow the directions carefully very carefully when taking this medication.

8. The surgery will begin at four p.m. tomorrow afternoon.

9. The surgical room is on fire.

10. The following reports were typed by the medical transcriptionist within the past hour radiology report, history and physical report, and pathology report.

Fill in the prefixes or suffixes for the meanings listed below.

cell	_____	between	_____
lack of	_____	new	_____
blood	_____		

COMPOSITION REINFORCEMENT

Directions: In the spaces provided, compose five paragraphs using the word mastery terms and applying the language skills you have studied. Complete and submit your work for this assignment according to your instructor's directions.

Paragraph 1: Write a paragraph using a series of three or more items and use commas correctly.

_____

_____

_____

_____

_____

_____

_____

Paragraph 2: Show an understanding of the proper use of dashes.

_____

_____

_____

_____

_____

_____

_____

Paragraph 3: Write a paragraph and use an exclamation point correctly.

_____
_____
_____
_____
_____
_____
_____

Paragraph 4: Write a paragraph using two of the word mastery terms correctly.

_____
_____
_____
_____
_____
_____
_____

Paragraph 5: Write a paragraph using correctly two of the word mastery terms that were not used in Paragraph 4.

_____
_____
_____
_____
_____
_____
_____

Name: _____   Date: _____

COLLABORATIVE RESEARCH

Directions: In small groups, work together to locate five recent articles from newspapers, magazines, the library, or the Internet that relate to medical ethics, medical cases, medical documents, medical terminology, or the medical profession that you did not use in previous chapters. List the source and date of each article and summarize each of the articles in the spaces provided below.

Complete and submit your work for this assignment according to your instructor's directions.

1. Source, date, and summary of article:

_____

_____

_____

_____

_____

_____

_____

2. Source, date, and summary of article:

_____

_____

_____

_____

_____

_____

_____

3. Source, date, and summary of article:

_____

_____

_____

_____

_____

_____

4. Source, date, and summary of article:

_____

_____

_____

_____

_____

_____

5. Source, date, and summary of article:

_____

_____

_____

_____

_____

_____

Directions: Complete all learning activities in this chapter and read all steps before beginning the transcription exercises.

1. Review the format for modified block letters with mixed punctuation and medical documents in the reference manual.

2. Retrieve the file from the student CD for each document to be transcribed.
   • For Document 1, open TE18-1, a radiologist's report for Great Lakes Associates in Radiology and Imaging.

   • For Document 2, open TE18-2, a letterhead for Great Lakes Associates in Radiology and Imaging.

3. Remember to use the Save As feature and an appropriate filename for each document.

4. Insert the information for Document 1 that is dictated on the student CD. Use the modified block style letter with mixed punctuation for Document 2.

5. Transcribe all the medical documents from the student CD in acceptable form using the current date unless another date is given.

6. Proofread, spell-check, and submit all documents to your instructor for approval.

CHAPTER *Checkpoints*

Upon completion of the various learning activities in this chapter, you should be able to meet the objectives listed at the beginning of this chapter. If you feel you cannot answer "yes" to all of the statements listed below, consult your instructor.

Directions: *Place a check mark (✔) in the box for all that apply.*

☐ I can define and use the word mastery terms presented in this chapter.

☐ I can apply the prefixes and suffixes presented in this chapter.

☐ I can compose paragraphs in acceptable form utilizing the word mastery terms and language skills presented in this chapter.

☐ I can use my researching, writing, and communication skills correctly.

☐ I can transcribe medical documents in acceptable form.

Answers to Word Mastery Self-Check

1. Her doctor thought the pain was from **degenerative** arthritis.
2. Those who suffer from **spondylolisthesis** can often find relief from pain by visiting a chiropractor for adjustment of the spine.
3. Many children are checked for **levoscoliosis** when they visit their pediatricians for a yearly physical.
4. Her **acute** headache even caused her to have vision problems.
5. Although she was scared to have the **magnetic resonance imaging** performed, she discovered there was no pain involved.
6. **Arthritic** pain occurs in many senior adults as the body ages.
7. Arthritic **spurring** causes severe pain.
8. The doctor prescribed calcium to his patient to help prevent **demineralization** of her bones.
9. The **aorta** is an artery in the heart.
10. When the doctor looked at the x-rays, he could see the **apophyseal** joints.

Answers to Language Skills Self-Check

1. The interns will need to attend the orientation meeting at three o'clock.
2. Check the patient's blood pressure, temperature, and other vital signs—these were the procedures she was to follow. (No corrections needed.)
3. If—and only if—you must leave the class, be sure you ask someone to take notes for you.
4. This is an emergency!
5. The following students will be graduating from the program: Tomas Medina, Margarita Flores, and Oki Beppu.
6. Anatomy, pathology, and pharmacology—these courses need to be taken before you proceed with the medical transcription course.
7. I cannot stress that you follow the directions carefully—very carefully—when taking this medication.
8. The surgery will begin at 4 p.m. tomorrow afternoon.
9. The surgical room is on fire!
10. The following reports were typed by the medical transcriptionist within the past hour: radiology report, history and physical report, and pathology report.

cell	**-cyte**
lack of	**de-**
blood	**hemato-**
between	**inter-**
new	**neo-**

Student's Name: _____

Instructor's Name: _____

Class: _____

	Date Work Submitted	Grades (Determined by Instructor)
Composition Reinforcement	_____	_____
Collaborative Research	_____	_____
Transcription Exercises	_____	_____
	_____	_____
	_____	_____
	_____	_____

Instructor's Comments Regarding Work or Suggestions for Improvement:

_____

_____

_____

_____

_____

_____

_____

_____

Medical Transcriptionist Job Description, Operative Report, and Dental Report

Typically, family dentistry has focused on the care and treatment of the gums and teeth. Like other fields of medicine, dentists today also specialize. Specialists include the endodonist, who does root canal work; the oral surgeon, who specializes in jaw surgery and extractions; the orthodontist, who is skilled in straightening teeth; the pedodontist, who specializes in dental care for children; the periodontist, who treats gum disease; and the prosthodontist, who makes dentures and artificial teeth.

LEARNING OBJECTIVES

After completing all the learning activities in this chapter, you will be able to:

Define and use the word mastery terms presented in this chapter correctly.

Apply the medical prefixes and suffixes presented in this chapter.

Apply previously learned grammar and punctuation skills.

Compose paragraphs in acceptable form utilizing the word mastery terms and language skills presented in this chapter.

Utilize your researching, writing, and communication skills correctly in a collaborative research activity.

Transcribe medical documents in acceptable form.

Directions: Learn the definition for each word and how to spell it correctly. Examples of word mastery terms used during the transcription process are given below.

periodontal

Definition: the area around a tooth

Example: Periodontal comes from *peri*, meaning surrounding; *odonto*, meaning teeth; and *al*, meaning pertaining to.

endotracheal

Definition: within the trachea, the main trunk by which air passes to and from the lungs

Example: An endotracheal tube may be placed into the trachea through the mouth to establish an airway.

subgingival

Definition: beneath the gingiva, the teeth-bearing portion of the gum

Example: Proper brushing, flossing, and use of a dental irrigating device will help to avoid subgingival dental problems.

calculus

Definition: an abnormal hardening composed of mineral salts occurring within the body; stones

Example: To ensure good dental health, calculus must periodically be cleaned from teeth.

supragingival

Definition: above the gingiva, the teeth-bearing portion of the gum

Example: Supragingival and subgingival disease is treated by a periodontist.

Titan scaler

Definition: a dental instrument used to remove calculus from teeth

Example: A Titan scaler was used by the hygienist to scrape calculus from the patient's teeth.

prophylaxis

Definition: prevention of disease; preventative treatment

Example: Dental prophylaxis is the description of the procedure used on insurance forms when patients have their teeth cleaned.

sulci

Definition: the plural of sulcus; grooves or furrows

Example: The spaces between the surface of teeth and the linings on the free surface of the gingiva are referred to as gingival sulci.

lactated Ringers	*Definition:*	a blood serum substitute used to replace blood lost in emergencies
	Example:	Lactated Ringers is a solution for blood or serum.
Novocain	*Definition:*	an anesthetic
	Example:	The dentist gave the patient an injection of Novocain prior to extracting the tooth.
debris	*Definition:*	the remains of anything broken down or destroyed; fragments
	Example:	The patient rinsed her mouth to remove any debris from the cleaning of her teeth.
cuspids	*Definition:*	a conical-pointed tooth, especially one situated between the lateral incisor and the first premolar
	Example:	Sarah Katherine did not like having her cuspids removed.
cysts	*Definition:*	a closed sac having a distinct membrane and developing abnormally in a cavity or structure of the body
	Example:	The dentist found several cysts within the area of the maxillary cuspids.
pericoronal	*Definition:*	around the crown of the tooth
	Example:	There were several cysts in the pericoronal area in the patient's teeth.

Directions: Complete each sentence by filling in one of the word mastery terms. You may check your answers at the end of this chapter.

1. Most people fear going to the dentist because of the _____ work that must be done.

2. Sometimes it feels very awkward having the _____ tube in your mouth as the dentist examines your teeth.

3. We should go to our dentists every six months for_____, which can prevent tooth decay.

4. When the dental hygienist cleans your teeth, she scrapes the _____ of your teeth to remove the buildup of calculus.

5. Because people cannot take the pain involved with dental work, dentists use _____, which eliminates the sensation of pain.

6. When you have your teeth cleaned, the dental hygienist removes the _____ from your teeth.

7. _____ disease is found around the upper gum area.

8. _____ disease is found around the lower gum area.

9. As your hygienist cleans your teeth, she uses a(n) _____ _____ to remove the calculus.

10. You can clean the _____ from your mouth by rinsing as your teeth are cleaned.

Directions: Knowing various prefixes and suffixes used within the medical fields will help you become more familiar with the meanings of medical terms. Some of the prefixes and suffixes listed below are used in the word mastery terms you are studying within the chapter. Learn each prefix or suffix and its meaning.

Prefix or Suffix	Meaning
endo-	within
gingivo-	gums
-graphy	process of recording
-itis	inflammation
-logy	study of
-oma	tumor
peri-	around, surrounding
-plasty	surgical repair
sub-	under, below
supra-	above, over

Directions: These examples include language skills presented in the previous chapters. You may want to refer to the reference manual for a review before you begin.

Make any corrections in the following sentences. Then check your answers at the end of this chapter.

1. We need to attend meetings in Charlotte, North Carolina, Charleston, South Carolina, and Miami, Florida.

2. In 1999 45 dentists graduated from the dental school in our state.

3. My dentist said, "that he wanted me to floss my teeth every day."

4. She asked what I wanted to eat for dinner.

5. I will have to have another checkup with my dentist in the Fall.

6. The dentist said I want to see you back for your checkup in six months.

7. He had attended school in Raleigh North Carolina Tallahassee Florida and Atlanta Georgia.

8. On page 45 11 items were omitted in the report.

9. The medical secretary asked, "If I wanted to make an appointment."

10. The dental assistant said that she could not locate my files but would return my call as soon as she found it.

Fill in the prefixes or suffixes for the meanings listed below.

gums   _____

around, surrounding   _____

under, below   _____

tumor   _____

surgical repair   _____

COMPOSITION REINFORCEMENT

Directions: In the spaces provided, compose five paragraphs using the word mastery terms and applying the language skills you have studied. Complete and submit your work for this assignment according to your instructor's directions.

Paragraph 1: Write a paragraph using two of the word mastery terms correctly.

_____

_____

_____

_____

_____

_____

_____

Paragraph 2: Show an understanding of the proper use of quotation marks with a direct quote.

_____

_____

_____

_____

_____

_____

_____

Paragraph 3: Show an understanding of the proper use of commas and semicolons when giving a listing of three or more cities and states.

_____

_____

_____

_____

_____

_____

Paragraph 4: Write a paragraph correctly using two of the word mastery terms that were not used in Paragraph 1.

_____

_____

_____

_____

_____

_____

Paragraph 5: Explain the difference between the terms **subgingival** and **supragingival**.

_____

_____

_____

_____

_____

_____

COLLABORATIVE RESEARCH

Directions: In small groups, work together to locate five recent articles from newspapers, magazines, the library, or the Internet that relate to medical/dental ethics, medical/dental cases, medical/dental documents, medical/dental terminology, or the medical/dental profession that you did not use in previous chapters. List the source and date of each article and summarize each of the articles in the spaces provided below.

Complete and submit your work for this assignment according to your instructor's directions.

1. Source, date, and summary of article:

_____

_____

_____

_____

_____

_____

_____

2. Source, date, and summary of article:

_____

_____

_____

_____

_____

_____

_____

_____

3. Source, date, and summary of article:

_____

_____

_____

_____

_____

_____

_____

4. Source, date, and summary of article:

_____

_____

_____

_____

_____

_____

_____

5. Source, date, and summary of article:

_____

_____

_____

_____

_____

_____

_____

Directions: Complete all learning activities in this chapter and read all steps before beginning the transcription exercises.

1. Review the format for reports and medical documents in the reference manual.

2. Retrieve the file from the student's CD for each document to be transcribed.
   - Print Document 1 on plain paper.
   - For Document 2, open TE19-2, an Operative Report.

- Print Document 3 on plain paper.

3. For Document 2, remember to use the Save As feature and an appropriate filename.

4. Insert the information for Document 2 that is dictated on the student's CD.

5. Transcribe all the medical documents from the student's CD in acceptable form using the current date unless another date is given.

6. Proofread, spell-check, and submit all documents to your instructor for approval.

CHAPTER *Checkpoints*

Upon completion of the various learning activities in this chapter, you should be able to meet the objectives listed at the beginning of this chapter. If you feel you cannot answer "yes" to all of the statements listed below, consult your instructor.

Directions: *Place a check mark (✓) in the box for all that apply.*

☐ I can define and use the word mastery terms presented in this chapter.

☐ I can apply the grammar and punctuation rules learned in previous chapters.

☐ I can use my researching, writing, and communication skills correctly.

☐ I can apply the prefixes and suffixes presented in this chapter.

☐ I can compose paragraphs in acceptable form utilizing the word mastery terms and language skills presented in this chapter.

☐ I can transcribe medical documents in acceptable form.

Answers to Word Mastery Self-Check

1. Most people fear going to the dentist because of the **periodontal** work that must be done.
2. Sometimes it feels very awkward having the **endotracheal** tube in your mouth as the dentist examines your teeth.
3. We should go to our dentists every six months for **prophylaxis**, which can prevent tooth decay.
4. When the dental hygienist cleans your teeth, she scrapes the **sulci** of your teeth to remove the buildup of calculus.
5. Because people cannot take the pain involved with dental work, dentists use **Novocain**, which eliminates the sensation of pain.
6. When you have your teeth cleaned, the dental hygienist removes the **calculus** from your teeth.
7. **Supragingival** disease is found around the upper gum area.
8. **Subgingival** disease is found around the lower gum area.
9. As your hygienist cleans your teeth, she uses a **Titan scaler** to remove the calculus.
10. You can clean the **debris** from your mouth by rinsing as your teeth are cleaned.

Answers to Language Skills Self-Check

1. We need to attend meetings in Charlotte, North Carolina; Charleston, South Carolina; and Miami, Florida.
2. In 1999, 45 dentists graduated from the dental school in our state.
3. My dentist said that he wanted me to floss my teeth every day.
4. She asked what I wanted to eat for dinner. (No corrections needed.)
5. I will have to have another checkup with my dentist in the fall.
6. The dentist said, "I want to see you back for your checkup in six months."
7. He had attended school in Raleigh, North Carolina; Tallahassee, Florida; and Atlanta, Georgia.
8. On page 45, 11 items were omitted in the report.
9. The medical secretary asked if I wanted to make an appointment.
10. The dental assistant said that she could not locate my files but would return my call as soon as she found it. (No corrections needed.)

gums	**gingivo-**
around, surrounding	**peri-**
under, below	**sub-**
tumor	**-oma**
surgical repair	**-plasty**

Student's Name: _____

Instructor's Name: _____

Class: _____

	Date Work Submitted	Grades (Determined by Instructor)
Composition Reinforcement	_____	_____
Collaborative Research	_____	_____
Transcription Exercises	_____	_____
	_____	_____
	_____	_____

Instructor's Comments Regarding Work or Suggestions for Improvement:

_____

_____

_____

_____

_____

_____

_____

_____

_____

chapter

Admission Letter, Pathology Report, and Discharge Summary

As a transcriptionist in a hospital, you will process all of the hospital's correspondence and medical reports. If an error is detected in a document once it has left the transcription department, multiple forms must be completed and distributed to all the doctors needing a copy of the amended document. Therefore, accuracy is essential.

LEARNING OBJECTIVES

After completing all the learning activities in this chapter, you will be able to:

Define and use the word mastery terms presented in this chapter correctly.

Apply the medical prefixes and suffixes presented in this chapter.

Apply grammar and punctuation rules learned in previous chapters.

Compose paragraphs in acceptable form utilizing the word mastery terms and language skills presented in this chapter.

Utilize your researching, writing, and communication skills correctly in a collaborative research activity.

Transcribe medical documents in acceptable form.

Directions: Learn the definition for each word and how to spell it correctly. Examples of word mastery terms used during the transcription process are given below.

omental	*Definition:*	pertaining to a fold of the cavity of the abdomen
	Example:	The omental region is divided into the greater and lesser omental areas.
mesentery	*Definition:*	one or more vertebrate membranes that consist of a double fold of the peritoneum and invest the intestines and their appendages
	Example:	The elderly lady had several mesentery problems.
peritoneal	*Definition:*	pertaining to the membrane wall lining the walls of the abdominal and pelvic cavities
	Example:	Acute and chronic renal failure are among the most common indications for peritoneal dialysis.
metastatic	*Definition:*	the transfer of disease from one organ or part to another not directly connected with it
	Example:	The cancerous tumors were removed, but there were metastatic possibilities that they could recur.
adenocarcinoma	*Definition:*	cancerous tumor of a gland
	Example:	Adenocarcinoma tumor cells form recognizable glandular structures.
pancreas	*Definition:*	a large, elongated gland located behind the stomach
	Example:	The pancreas produces insulin.
nodule	*Definition:*	a solid node that can be detected by touch
	Example:	A surfer's nodule can occur on the bony area of the feet or legs and is the result of kneeling on surfboards.
bisected	*Definition:*	cut into two parts
	Example:	Myrna bisected the tissue for microscopic study.
aneurysm	*Definition:*	a pouch formed by the localized abnormal relation of the wall on an artery
	Example:	The most common site for an arterial aneurysm is the aorta.

carotid	*Definition:*	the principal artery of the neck
	Example:	A pulse may be taken by feeling the carotid artery.
angiographies	*Definition:*	radiography of vessels of the body
	Example:	The angiographies revealed artery blockage.

Directions: Complete each sentence by filling in one of the word mastery terms. You may check your answers at the end of this chapter.

1. The doctors said her cancer was _____ because it had spread to other parts of her body.

2. Although we can live without our spleen, we cannot live without our _____.

3. In many biology classes, students _____ tissues from frogs.

4. A(n) _____ can occur in the heart or in the brain.

5. Her physician wanted to take _____ to determine if she had blockage in her arteries.

6. _____ dialysis may be required with chronic renal failure.

7. Abigail had a cancerous tumor of the gland, which is called a(n) _____.

8. John felt his _____ artery to see how fast his pulse was after he exercised.

9. A(n) _____ had formed on one of his knees from kneeling to pray daily.

10. The surgeon wanted to examine the _____ area in his abdomen.

Directions: Knowing various prefixes and suffixes used within the medical fields will help you become more familiar with the meanings of medical terms. Some of the prefixes and suffixes listed below are used in the word mastery terms you are studying within the chapter. Learn each prefix or suffix and its meaning.

Prefix or Suffix	Meaning
angio-	vessel
dys-	bad, painful, difficult
hystero-	uterus, womb
-megaly	enlargement
meta-	beyond, change
-ostomy	new opening
patho-	disease
-phobia	fear
-stenosis	narrowing, stricture
-tomy	incision

Directions: These examples include language skills presented in the previous chapters. You may want to refer to the reference manual for a review before you begin.

Make any corrections in the following sentences. Then check your answers at the end of this chapter.

1. Toby Pennell dean of the medical college was to speak at the commencement exercises.

2. *Journal Of The American Association For Medical Transcription* is an excellent bimonthly journal.

3. You will need to complete the following steps 1. Read the information in your chapter. 2. Study the word mastery terms, medical prefixes and medical suffixes. 3. Review the rules in the language skills section from previous chapters.

4. Your application for graduation will amount to twenty-five dollars ($25).

5. The test will cover chapters two and three.

6. *The Journal of the American Association for Medical Transcription* is a publication many medical transcriptionists read.

7. Be sure to read all the material and complete all the work in Chapters Seventeen to Twenty before you take your next test.

8. Here is the procedure to follow before you go to Part 4: (1) Complete the Proofreading Assignment, (2) Take the written test, and (3) Take the transcription test.

9. If you study you will do well on your test however if you do not study you will probably not score as well.

10. All the material in this textbook has been designed to help you be successful in transcribing proofreading and correcting documents.

Fill in the prefixes or suffixes for the meanings listed below.

incision	_____	uterus, womb	_____
fear	_____	disease	_____
enlargement	_____		

COMPOSITION REINFORCEMENT

Directions: In the spaces provided, compose five paragraphs using the word mastery terms and applying the language skills you have studied. Complete and submit your work for this assignment according to your instructor's directions.

Paragraph 1: Write a paragraph using two of the word mastery terms correctly.

_____

_____

_____

_____

_____

_____

_____

Paragraph 2: Show an understanding of the proper use of numbers with a listing within a sentence.

_____

_____

_____

_____

_____

_____

_____

Paragraph 3: Show an understanding of the proper use of commas when setting off a word or words that rename the words they follow.

_____

_____

_____

_____

_____

_____

_____

Paragraph 4: Write a paragraph using correctly two of the word mastery terms that were not used in Paragraph 1.

_____

_____

_____

_____

_____

_____

_____

Paragraph 5: Show an understanding of the proper use of expressing monetary amounts.

_____

_____

_____

_____

_____

_____

_____

COLLABORATIVE RESEARCH

Directions: In small groups, work together to locate five recent articles from newspapers, magazines, the library, or the Internet that relate to medical ethics, medical cases, medical documents, medical terminology, or the medical profession that you did not use in previous chapters. List the source and date of each article and summarize each of the articles in the spaces provided below.

Complete and submit your work for this assignment according to your instructor's directions.

1. Source, date, and summary of article:

_____

_____

_____

_____

_____

_____

_____

2. Source, date, and summary of article:

_____

_____

_____

_____

_____

_____

_____

3. Source, date, and summary of article:

_____

_____

_____

_____

_____

_____

4. Source, date, and summary of article:

_____

_____

_____

_____

_____

_____

_____

5. Source, date, and summary of article:

_____

_____

_____

_____

_____

_____

_____

Directions: Complete all learning activities in this chapter and read all steps before beginning the transcription exercises.

1. Review the format for block style letters with mixed punctuation and medical documents in the reference manual.

2. Retrieve the file from the student's CD for each document to be transcribed.
   - For Document 1, open TE20-1, letterhead for Good Fellowship Community Hospital.
   - For Document 2, open TE20-2, a Surgical Pathology Report.

   - For Document 3, open TE20-3, a Discharge Summary.

3. Remember to use the Save As feature and an appropriate filename for each document.

4. Use the block style letter with mixed punctuation for Document 1; insert the information for Documents 2 and 3 that is dictated on the student's CD.

5. Transcribe all the medical documents on the student's CD in acceptable form using the current date unless another date is given.

6. Proofread, spell-check, and submit all documents to your instructor for approval.

CHAPTER *Checkpoints*

Upon completion of the various learning activities in this chapter, you should be able to meet the objectives listed at the beginning of this chapter. If you feel you cannot answer "yes" to all of the statements listed below, consult your instructor.

Directions: *Place a check mark (✓) in the box for all that apply.*

☐ I can define and use the word mastery terms presented in this chapter.

☐ I can apply the grammar and punctuation rules learned in previous chapters.

☐ I can use my researching, writing, and communication skills correctly.

☐ I can apply the prefixes and suffixes presented in this chapter.

☐ I can compose paragraphs in acceptable form utilizing the word mastery terms and language skills presented in this chapter.

☐ I can transcribe medical documents in acceptable form.

ANSWER KEY FOR *Self-Checks*

Answers to Word Mastery Self-Check

1. The doctors said her cancer was **metastatic** because it had spread to other parts of her body.
2. Although we can live without our spleen, we cannot live without our **pancreas**.
3. In many biology classes, students **bisected** tissues from frogs.
4. An **aneurysm** can occur in the heart or in the brain.
5. Her physician wanted to take **angiographies** to determine if she had blockage in her arteries.
6. **Peritoneal** dialysis may be required with chronic renal failure.
7. Abigail had a cancerous tumor of the gland, which is called an **adenocarcinoma**.
8. John felt his **carotid** artery to see how fast his pulse was after he exercised.
9. A **nodule** had formed on one of his knees from kneeling to pray daily.
10. The surgeon wanted to examine the **omental** area in his abdomen.

Answers to Language Skills Self-Check

1. Toby Pennell, dean of the medical college, was to speak at the commencement exercises.
2. *Journal of the American Association for Medical Transcription* is an excellent bimonthly journal.
3. You will need to complete the following steps: (1) Read the information in your chapter. (2) Study the word mastery terms, medical prefixes, and medical suffixes. (3) Review the rules in the language skills section from previous chapters.
4. Your application for graduation will amount to twenty-five dollars ($25). (No corrections needed.)
5. The test will cover Chapters 2 and 3.
6. The *Journal of the American Association for Medical Transcription* is a publication many medical transcriptionists read.
7. Be sure to read all the material and complete all the work in Chapters 17 to 20 before you take your next test.
8. Here is the procedure to follow before you go to Part 4: (1) Complete the Proofreading Assignment, (2) Take the written test, and (3) Take the transcription test. (No corrections needed.)
9. If you study, you will do well on your test; however, if you do not study, you will probably not score as well.
10. All the material in this textbook has been designed to help you be successful in transcribing, proofreading, and correcting documents.

incision	**-tomy**	uterus, womb	**hystero-**
fear	**-phobia**	disease	**patho-**
enlargement	**-megaly**		

Complete the proofreading assignment on the following page to help prepare for the tests for Part 3. Follow your instructor's guidelines for completing this assignment. Take the written test and transcription test for Part 3 before proceeding to Part 4.

PROOFREADING ASSIGNMENT

Directions: This assignment should be completed following your instructor's guidelines. You may need to refer to the listing of the most commonly misspelled words as well as the listing of the most frequently misused words in business and industry. Both of these lists are located in your text-workbook. Refer to the list of proofreading marks in your text-workbook to be sure that you use the correct proofreading mark to indicate all errors that you find.

SPECIALTY FIELDS

As stated earlier in the text-workbook the legal and medical feilds are too areas that use machine transcription heavily. The information and dictation given in these last 8 chapters is just a brief introduction to these specialty fields. If you won't to seek employment as a transcriptionist in either of these fields you would need additional training.

There are other coarses that you can take to increase your skills in the legal or medical field. Prehaps your instructor can reccommend courses within your own institution of learning that would be beneficial for you to persue.

Student's Name: _____

Instructor's Name: _____

Class: _____

	Date Work Submitted	**Grades** (Determined by Instructor)
Composition Reinforcement	_____	_____
Collaborative Research	_____	_____
Transcription Exercises	_____	_____
	_____	_____
	_____	_____
	_____	_____
Proofreading Assignment	_____	_____

Instructor's Comments Regarding Work or Suggestions for Improvement:

_____

_____

_____

_____

_____

_____

_____

Part 4

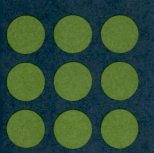

Dictation and Continuous Speech Recognition

In the previous chapters in the text-workbook, you have had the experience of transcribing dictation and should be familiar with how documents sound when dictated. This part has been included to give you the hands-on experience of dictating as well as transcribing information. Many business people do not use dictating as a means of input because they have never been trained and do not feel confident in using the equipment. After you have had the opportunity in this part to dictate and transcribe material, you will want to use these skills as an efficient method of producing input when employed. You will also be given information about speech recognition. This concept uses the voice as the input device directly to the computer rather than dictating into a dictation/transcribing unit and then keying that information into the computer. Although you will be given information about this concept, you will not actually have hands-on experience using this technology.

1. Have all references or resource materials nearby to which you might need to refer.

2. Organize your thoughts by using an outline or brief notes of the material you wish to dictate.

3. Identify whether the dictation is a draft or final copy.

4. Discuss the format that is to be used such as report format or block letter format without punctuation.

5. Indicate if the document will need enclosures or copies.

6. Pronounce each word clearly and spell any word that has an unusual spelling or could be confused with another word. Example: Jean or Jon for John. Some letters sound alike; therefore, it might be helpful to give examples to ensure the transcriptionist understands.

    Example: Send the letter to P. T. Brown. Transcriptionist, that is "P" as in Peter and "T" as in Tom.

7. Use the expressions listed below to indicate the correct type of capitalization to use with the dictation:

    "Capital" means capitalize only the first letter of the next word.
    Example: (Capital) Columbia.

    "Caps" means capitalize the first letter of each major word in the following group of related words.
    Example: At our meeting, I will make the (Caps) Time Management speech to the (Caps) Fashion Institute.

    "All Caps" means use all capital letters in the next group of words until the originator says "End all caps."
    Example: This presentation is based on your (All caps) TIMESAVER (End all caps) calendar.

8. Dictate any punctuation or paragraph notations that might be helpful to the transcriptionist.

9. Indicate when a document is needed and whether it is a top priority document and needs to be transcribed quickly.

10. Be sure to state your name if the transcriptionist transcribes documents for many originators so she will know to whom to return the transcribed materials.

Directions: Read all of the steps before beginning these exercises.

1. Ask your instructor for a tape and the microphone to use with your machine transcription unit.

2. Because the dictation features vary depending on the brand of equipment you are using, you need to read the directions for operating the dictation features of your equipment listed in the operation manual that was enclosed with the transcription equipment when the equipment was purchased. If you do not have access to this manual, consult your instructor for a demonstration on how to properly use these features. If you have read the manual and still have concerns, consult your instructor.

3. Read the dictation guidelines listed on the previous page.

4. Review the language skills presented in the previous parts as well as the format for reports; you can refer to the reference manual in the back of this text-workbook.

5. Dictate and record onto a blank cassette the Transcription Practice Exercise that you used at the beginning of this course when you learned the listen, stop, and key process. (See pages 6–7.)

6. Dictate and record the information about continuous speech recognition, which appears on the following page. Note that the information does not include punctuation and paragraphing. You will have to supply these as you dictate. You will see how valuable the language skills you learned in previous chapters will be in completing this activity.

7. Read the additional information on continuous speech recognition in this part. Then research information on speech recognition by using the Internet, library, or office technology and/or equipment suppliers. The experience you gained in completing the collaborative research sections in the previous chapters will be valuable to you as you complete this activity. Write a two-page report on the future of speech recognition based on your research.

8. Dictate and record the report that summarizes what you learned from this research.

9. Transcribe the three documents that you dictated in acceptable report format. Use an appropriate title for each report.

10. Proofread, spell check, and submit the documents to your instructor for approval. You should also submit the tape that contains your dictation.

CONTINUOUS SPEECH RECOGNITION

Continuous speech recognition is an interesting concept that uses the human voice as an input device to the computer. If you want to use this concept you must have the proper software such as Dragon NaturallySpeaking L&H Voice Xpress and IBM ViaVoice. There are certain hardware and software requirements and you must enroll and train the software so it can adjust to your voice patterns. You will have to learn how to control the microphone dictate the text enter punctuation marks create breaks and delete errors. In addition to this training you also need to learn how to change and correct text create special characters and numbers make document changes and format text.

SPEECH TECHNOLOGY BASICS

After more than three decades of speculation about when speech recognition would be ready for prime time, continuous speech recognition (CSR) programs are now gaining popularity. With increased processor speeds, declining memory costs, and increased storage capacity, the modern personal computer can be a talking-typing machine.

The voice revolution began in the 1960s at IBM's famed Thomas J. Watson Research Center in Hawthorne, New York. IBM has long believed that the next jump in computer productivity would be caused by a voice-interface revolution. To this end, they committed three decades of research to study voice recognition. And they were not alone in their belief in the potential of voice-typing. While IBM was introducing its CSR software called ViaVoice, other companies were introducing CSR systems of their own.

- Dragon Systems impressed customers and analysts alike with Naturally Speaking.
- Lernout & Hauspie excited the crowd with VoiceXpress.
- Philips shined the spotlight on its FreeSpeech software.
- Dozens of smaller companies began to compete in the vigorous CSR marketplace.

The speech recognition software now available has progressed to the point that, when you talk, your computer can type your words accurately.

THE DREAM VERSUS THE REALITY

After the basics have been conquered, it takes additional time of dedicated practice to train your computer to understand your unique way of speaking. However, if you work at it, the results can be astounding. A typical person who spends adequate time training the software can expect to voice-type between 110 and 160 words per minute (wpm) with 90 to 98 percent accuracy.

HEALTH AND SAFETY ISSUES

Beyond the obvious input efficiencies for data entry, there are other reasons why businesses and schools are accepting voice. In February 1999, the Occupational Safety and Health Administration (OSHA) released a draft proposal on how employers must reduce repetitive strain injuries (RSI) and carpal tunnel syndrome in the workplace. OSHA calls these injuries work-related musculoskeletal disorders or WMSDs.

Speech represents a very important weapon in the battle against WMSDs. It is interesting to note that the sharp rise in WMSDs corresponds with the infusion of personal computers into the workplace starting in the mid 1980s While most WMSDs still occur in the manufacturing sector, office workers, using computer keyboards and the mouse, now suffer a significantly high portion of the WMSDs.

Speech dictation can help office workers who depend on keyboarding for their livelihoods. CSR systems can dramatically reduce the number of repetitive keystrokes these workers must make each day. Does this mean that some office workers can quit typing and use voice instead? For many suffering with WMSDs, the answer is an empathetic YES! For many carpal tunnel syndrome and RSI sufferers, a voice is a highly effective alternative to keyboarding.

BLENDING KEYBOARDING WITH VOICE INPUT

Most of us will continue to key part of the time and use our CSR software the rest of the time. It is, therefore, essential that keyboarding instructors continue to emphasize correct keying techniques and proper computer-office ergonomics.

In some situations it will be difficult, if not impossible, to use a CSR program; for instance, taking notes on your computer during a lecture or during a sales conference. Also, speaking all day to a computer can cause problems with your vocal cords. If you are going to use voice dictation software, you had better keep your water bottle handy, and give your voice a rest by keying with your hands every once in a while!

However, if you use a CSR program for even 50 percent of the time you spend in front of a computer, your chances of suffering severe WMSDs as you get older will diminish. So, if for no other reason than to avoid future long-term pain and suffering, a CSR program is well worth learning.

HARDWARE AND SOFTWARE REQUIREMENTS

With CSR systems, the faster your CPU and the greater your computer's memory capacity the better. Here is a lower-end computer configuration that can run most of today's popular CSR programs. Be sure to check your CSR software for exact specifications:

- 300 MHz Pentium II or higher
- 64 MB of RAM
- 200 MB or more of storage capacity
- CD-ROM for installation purposes
- Windows operating system
- CSR vendor approved sound card
- CSR software with approved microphone headset

With your hardware and software in place, you are ready to go to work. The dream fostered nearly 30 years ago of a voice interface for personal computers, has finally become a reality, and it's time for you to give it a try. But be prepared, it's going to take a little work!

CSR TRAINING

CSR software training can be divided into four parts that we will discuss in more detail:

1.	Enrollment and initial training	1–2 hours
2.	Training yourself in the basics	10–15 hours
3.	Training your computer to understand your voice	30+ hours
4.	Practice makes perfect	continual use

ENROLLMENT AND INITIAL TRAINING

Obviously, before you can do anything you must install your software, register yourself as a user, and make sure your microphone headset is working properly. Then you must proceed through a required initial training that will teach your computer to understand your unique accent and way of speaking.

INSTALLATION AND HEADSET ADJUSTMENT

The installation process is very straightforward. Read each screen and follow the instructions your software provides. You will be asked to enter your name, and then, with your headset on, your CSR program will walk you through several steps to make sure your headset is connected properly. The software will then adjust its audio settings to the volume of your voice.

MICROPHONE POSITION

CSR software works best when your headset is one-half to one inch away from your mouth and the tip of the microphone is placed slightly below your lower lip. It may also help to place the microphone slightly to one side of your mouth. You will need to experiment to find the best position. Once you find that position, be consistent! Place the microphone in the same position every time you use your CSR software.

If your microphone is too far away from your mouth, your recognition accuracy will be poor. If your microphone is too close to your mouth and nose, breathing errors will occur. A breathing error is caused by your breath brushing across the microphone and results in words like "the," "and," and "but" being printed across the screen.

Once your headset is working properly, you will be asked to read a series of sentences. The idea behind this training process is to record enough samples of your speech so the software can adjust to your voice patterns.

With most CSR programs, you will be recording sentences for 20 to 60 minutes. Don't despair. This is an important step that cannot be avoided. Do not skip this step if you ever hope to achieve any level of accuracy. Give your computer a chance to understand you!

Once you have trained your software, you need to learn the commands that will allow you to format and punctuate your document. These commands are similar to the commands that a person uses in dictating a document to be transcribed. The commands tell the software such things as where to place punctuation and when to begin a new paragraph. Each CSR program has its own set of commands. Some of the programs also have natural language commands that allow you to give the same command in several different ways.

Just as you have learned that practice is required to develop good transcription skills, you will find that practice is required to develop the skills needed to use voice recognition software effectively.

CHAPTER *Checkpoints*

Upon completion of the various learning activities in this chapter, you should be able to meet the objectives listed at the beginning of this chapter. If you feel you cannot answer "yes" to all of the statements listed below, consult your instructor.

Directions: *Place a check mark (✓) in the box for all that apply.*

☐ I can operate the dictating features of my equipment.

☐ I can transcribe documents in acceptable report form.

☐ I can organize my thoughts and dictate material using the dictating features of my equipment.

☐ I can use my researching, writing, and communication skills correctly.

☐ I can discuss continuous speech recognition.

Student's Name: _____

Instructor's Name: _____

Class: _____

	Date Work Submitted	Grades (Determined by Instructor)
Dictation and Transcription Exercises	_____	_____
	_____	_____
	_____	_____

Instructor's Comments Regarding Work or Suggestions for Improvement:

_____

_____

_____

_____

_____

_____

_____

_____

_____

_____

_____

_____

reference

m a n u a l

Symbol	Meaning	Example	After Revising
∧	insert text	*Traffic* Winn ∧ Engineering	Winn Traffic Engineering
∧	insert comma	Cincinnati ∧ Ohio	Cincinnati, Ohio
∨	insert apostrophe	Whitney∨s computer	Whitney's computer
=	insert hyphen	first=class service	first-class service
⊙	insert period	Meet me there ⊙	Meet me there.
⌒	close up	can⌒not	cannot
#	insert space	take#time	take time
tr or ∿	transpose	retreive	retrieve
lc	lowercase	QUALITY CONTROL	Quality Control
ℓ	delete	posstal	postal
/	replace	7 a.m. *p*	7 p.m.
_____	underline	Media Mess	Media Mess
≡ or cap	capitalize	transcription skills	Transcription Skills
sp	spell out	sp (6-)day vacation	six-day vacation
¶	new paragraph	...complete. ¶ Your work was excellent.	...complete. Your work was excellent.
... or stet	let stand; ignore the correction	just ~~in case~~ *stet*	just in case
⌐	move right	Please call before leaving the office.	Please call before leaving the office.
⌐	move left	⌐ Please call before leaving the office.	Please call before leaving the office.
♂	move copy as indicated	Madison's City (Budget)	Madison's City Budget
SS	single-space	SS { Your appointment is scheduled for tomorrow.	Your appointment is scheduled for tomorrow.
DS	double-space	DS { Your appointment is scheduled for tomorrow.	Your appointment is scheduled for tomorrow.

Proofreading is the reading of documents to locate and correct errors and inconsistencies. You must understand the principles of proofreading and apply proofreading techniques to produce acceptable documents. There are several tips that can help you become a better proofreader; some of these are listed below:

- Allow enough time to read carefully.
- Have resource materials such as an up-to-date dictionary and reference manuals handy when proofreading.
- Space some time between keying a document and immediately proofreading the document so your mind will not be "tricked" into seeing something you think you may have keyed.
- Check the document while it still appears on the screen before printing to save on printing costs.
- Proofread a document more than once to ensure that all errors have been found and corrected.
- Evaluate documents for typographical errors, grammar errors, content errors, and format errors.

absence	leisure
accommodate	maintenance
achievement	miscellaneous
acknowledgment	necessary
analysis	occasion
argument	occur
beneficial	occurrence
calendar	omission
column	parallel
committee	preferred
conscientious	privilege
convenience	pursue
definite	receipt
describe	receive
description	recommend
development	reference
experience	separate
extraordinary	similar
familiar	succeed
foreign	supersede
fulfill	transferred
grammar	truly
grateful	undoubtedly
guarantee	unnecessary
judgment	writing

accede	to comply with
exceed	to surpass
accept	to receive
except	to exclude
ad	abbreviated form of advertisement
add	to make an addition
adapt	to adjust
adept	skillful
adopt	to take
addition	a joining
edition	a version of a publication
adjoin	next to
adjourn	to end a meeting
advice	a recommendation
advise	to give a recommendation
affect	(v.) to influence, to change
effect	(v.) to bring about
	(n.) a result
aid	(v.) to help
	(n.) a form of help
aide	a person who helps
all together	in a group
altogether	thoroughly
among	used when referring to three or more
between	used when referring to two
a lot	a great deal
allot	to assign a share of something
all ready	a group is prepared
already	previously
assistance	help
assistants	helpers
capital	(n.) money; seat of government
	(adj.) main or most important
capitol	(n.) a building in which government meets

choose	to select
chose	past tense of the verb choose
cite	to state or quote
sight	vision; a scene
site	a place
coarse	rough
course	a subject of study
complement	to complete
compliment	to give praise
consul	a government official
council	an assembly
counsel	(v.) to give advice
	(n.) a person who gives advice
correspondence	business documents
correspondents	people to whom documents are sent or received
disburse	to distribute funds
disperse	to scatter
disinterested	not biased
uninterested	lacking interest
eligible	qualified
illegible	unreadable
eminent	important
imminent	ready to happen
farther	refers to distance
further	in greater detail
formally	in a ceremonious manner
formerly	previously
forth	forward
fourth	after third
its	possessive form of it
it's	contraction of it is
lead	(v.) to guide
	(n.) metal
led	past tense of lead

loose	(v.) to release
	(adj.) not tight
lose	(v.) to suffer a loss
maybe	perhaps
may be	a verb tense of two words
passed	past tense of the verb pass
past	time gone by
patience	calmness
patients	people who receive medical treatment
peace	(n.) calm
piece	(v.) to join
	(n.) a part
personal	private
personnel	pertaining to work staff
peruse	to read
pursue	to go after
precede	to go before
proceed	to advance
principal	(n.) a leader; money
	(adj.) main
principle	law
quiet	not noisy
quit	to stop
quite	entirely
respectfully	in a special manner
respectively	in the order given
right	(adj.) correct
	(n.) a privilege
rite	(n.) a ceremony
write	(v). to inscribe
stationary	not movable
stationery	writing paper
their	belong to them
there	in a certain place

to	toward
too	also; to a certain degree
two	one and one
ware	goods
wear	to put on
where	at a certain place
weather	conditions in the atmosphere
whether	if
whose	possessive form of who
who's	contraction of who is
want	desire
won't	contraction of will not
your	belonging to you
you're	contraction of you are

The U.S. Postal Service recommends that envelopes be addressed using a format that can be sorted by optical character readers (OCRs) and bar code sorters (BCSs). The OCRs and BCSs increase the speed, efficiency, and accuracy of processing your mail while keeping postal operating costs down.

Envelopes must be the right size and shape to speed with ease through the equipment, and they must be electronically "readable." Readable mail is addressed so that it can be "read" by the OCR. The eye of the OCR starts reading from the bottom line and is designed to search for the city, state, and ZIP Code first. If the address is located within the following boundaries, the OCR will have no trouble finding it:

- Sides of rectangle—1" in from the right and left edges
- Bottom of rectangle—⅝" up from the bottom edge
- Top of rectangle—2¾" up from the bottom edge

The lines of the address should appear in the order shown below. The address should be as complete as possible, including apartment or suite numbers and the proper delivery designations such as street, road, avenue, and so on. Set a tab approximately one-half inch left of the center of the envelope. Space down to Line 14 from the top edge of the envelope. Begin keying at the tab.

The address should be keyed using all caps and no punctuation. The two-letter state and province abbreviations listed should be used along with the correct ZIP Code and keyed one space following the state abbreviation. Remember to key special notations (HOLD FOR ARRIVAL and PERSONAL) in all caps a double space below the return address. Key mailing notations (SPECIAL DELIVERY, REGISTERED MAIL, etc.) in all caps a double space below the postage position.

Envelope

Alabama, AL	Montana, MT
Alaska, AK	Nebraska, NE
Arizona, AZ	Nevada, NV
Arkansas, AR	New Hampshire, NH
California, CA	New Jersey, NJ
Colorado, CO	New Mexico, NM
Connecticut, CT	New York, NY
Delaware, DE	North Carolina, NC
District of Columbia, DC	North Dakota, ND
Florida, FL	Ohio, OH
Georgia, GA	Oklahoma, OK
Guam, GU	Oregon, OR
Hawaii, HI	Pennsylvania, PA
Idaho, ID	Puerto Rico, PR
Illinois, IL	Rhode Island, RI
Indiana, IN	South Carolina, SC
Iowa, IA	South Dakota, SD
Kansas, KS	Tennessee, TN
Kentucky, KY	Texas, TX
Louisiana, LA	Utah, UT
Maine, ME	Vermont, VT
Maryland, MD	Virgin Islands, VI
Massachusetts, MA	Virginia, VA
Michigan, MI	Washington, WA
Minnesota, MN	West Virginia, WV
Mississippi, MS	Wisconsin, WI
Missouri, MO	Wyoming, WY

This section of the Reference Manual contains sample documents to use as guides when completing your work. Refer to these documents as needed.

Unbound Report, page 1

DS x 3

DS **TRENDS FOR BUSINESS DRESS** 14 point

DS Casual dress in the workplace has become widely accepted. According to a national study conducted by Schoenholtz & Associates in 1995, a majority of the companies surveyed allowed employees to dress casually one day a week, usually Fridays (Tartt, 1995, p. 23). The trend continued to climb as shown by the 1997 survey by Schoenholtz & Associates. Fifty-eight percent of office workers surveyed were allowed to dress casually for work every day, and 92 percent of the offices allowed employees to dress casually occasionally (Sutphin, 2000, p. 10).

Decline in Trend

The trend to dress casually that started in the early 1990s may be shifting, states Susan Monaghan (2000, p. 34):

Although a large number of companies are allowing casual attire every day or only on Fridays, a current survey revealed a decline of 10 percent in 1999 when compared to the same survey conducted in 1998. Some experts predict the new trend for business dress codes will be a dress up day every week.

What accounts for this decline in companies permitting casual dress? Several reasons may include:

1. Confusion of what business casual is with employees slipping into dressing too casually (work jeans, faded tee-shirts, old sneakers, and improperly fitting clothing).

2. Casual dress does not portray the adopted corporate image of the company.

3. Employees are realizing that promotion decisions are affected by a professional appearance.

1" LM

1" RM

At least 1"

Unbound Report, page 2

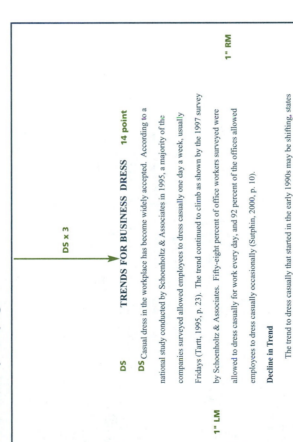

0.5" TM

2

DS

Guidelines for Business Dress

Companies are employing image consultants to teach employees what is appropriate business casual and to plan the best business attire to project the corporate image. Erica Gilreath (2000), the author of *Casual Dress*, a guidebook on business

DS

casual, provides excellent advice on how to dress casually and still command the power

DS

needed for business success. She presents the following advice to professionals:

DS

- Do not wear any clothing that is designed for recreational or sports activities, e.g., cargo pants or pants with elastic waist.

- Invest the time in pressing khakis and shirts or pay the price for professional dry cleaning. Wrinkled clothing does not enhance one's credibility.

- Do not wear sneakers.

- Be sure clothing fits properly. Avoid baggy clothes or clothes that are too tight.

In summary, energetic employees working to climb the corporate ladder will need to plan their dress carefully. If business casual is appropriate, it's best to consult the experts on business casual to ensure a professional image.

Block Letter Style with Open Punctuation

Professional Office Consultants, Inc.
584 Castro St.
San Francisco, CA 94114-2201
415-555-8725
415-555-8775 (FAX)

Dateline — January 17, 200-

QS

Letter address — Ms. Amanda Castillo, Office Manager
TeleNet Corporation
24 Technology Dr.
Irvine, CA 92865-9845

DS

Salutation — Dear Ms. Castillo

DS

Body — Thank you for selecting Professional Office Consultants, Inc. to assist with the setup of your new corporate office. You asked us for a recommendation for formatting business letters. We highly recommend the block letter style because it is easy to read, economical to produce, and efficient.

This letter is keyed in block format. As you can see, all lines begin at the left margin. Most letters can be keyed using default side margins and then centered vertically on the page for attractive placement. The block letter format is easy to key because tabs are not required.

We think that you will be happy using the block letter format. Over 80 percent of businesses today are using this same style.

DS

Complimentary close — Sincerely

QS

Writer's Title — Anderson Cline
OA & CIS Consultant

DS

Reference initials — tr

Modified Block Letter Style with Mixed Punctuation

IMAGE MAKERS
5131 Moss Springs Road
Columbia, SC 29209-4768
(803) 555-0127

October 27, 200-

Ms. Mary Bernard, President
Bernard Image Consultants
4927 Stuart Ave.
Baton Rouge, LA 70808-3519

Dear Ms. Bernard:

The format of this letter is called modified block. Modified block format differs from block format in that the date, complimentary close, and the signature lines are positioned at the center point.

Paragraphs may be blocked, as this letter illustrates, or they may be indented from the left margin. We suggest you block paragraphs when you use modified block style so that an additional tab setting is not needed. However, some people who use modified block format prefer indented paragraphs.

Although modified block format is very popular, we recommend that you use it only for those customers who request this letter style. Otherwise, we urge you to use block format, which is more efficient, as your standard style.

Both formats are illustrated in the enclosed *Image Makers Format Guide*. Please note that the block format is labeled "computer compatible."

Sincerely,

Patrick R. Ray
Communication Consultant

tr

Enclosure notation — Enclosure

Copy notation — c Scot Carl, Account Manager

Second Page of Two-Page Letter

Mr. Jason Artis
Page 2
April 9, 200-

DS

You will need to perform the following steps:

1. Review the sample projects and proposed guidelines.
2. Determine the specific responsibilities of the project manager and put these in writing.

Thank you, Mr. Artis, for your cooperation. It is always a pleasure working with you.

Very truly yours

.5"

Simplified Letter Format

Becker Information Services

1780 Whitemont Drive, Suite 200
Brookfield, WI 53005-1780
Telephone: (414) 555-0126   Fax (414) 555-0136

October 11, 20--

QS

Mr. Jeffrey S. Hayes
Town and Rural Bank
125 South Market Street
Chattanooga, TN 37344-1008

DS

CUSTOMIZED SEMINARS FOR FIRST-TIME INVESTORS

DS

As a valued client of Becker Information Services, Inc., you are the first in your area to receive our announcement brochure of our offering of customized seminars for first-time investors. These seminars are intended for your sponsorship to a select group of your customers.

DS

We would like to meet with you to discuss the feasibility of your sponsorship. Briefly, we would like to discuss the specific topics you would want presented and a profile of the "typical" customer you would invite as your guest. With this information, we can assure you that the program you approve will be just right for a first-time investor banking at Town and Rural Bank.

After our initial meeting and your approval of the program, you can turn the entire operation of planning and presenting over to Becker Information Services. We will handle all the details as we have done for you in the past.

I will call you early next week to set up an appointment that is convenient for you. In the meantime, if you have questions, please give me a call at 555-0126.

QS

Cindy Roeske Becker
Vice President, Sales

DS

CRB/jsv

DS

Enclosure

Certificate of Notary

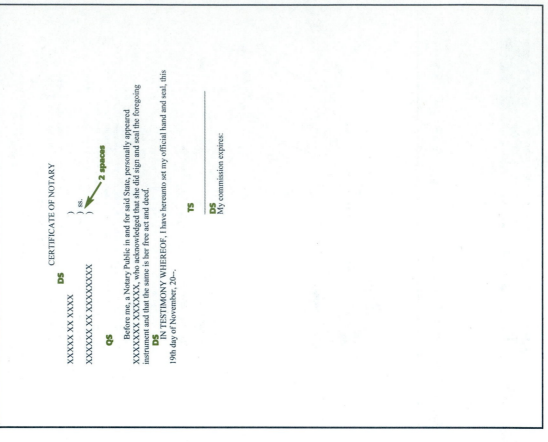

CERTIFICATE OF NOTARY

DS

XXXXX XX XXXX   )
) ss.
XXXXXX XX XXXXXXXX   )

QS   **2 spaces**

Before me, a Notary Public in and for said State, personally appeared XXXXXXX XXXXXX, who acknowledged that she did sign and seal the foregoing instrument and that the same is her free act and deed.

DS

IN TESTIMONY WHEREOF, I have hereunto set my official hand and seal, this 19th day of November, 20--.

TS

_____

DS

My commission expires:

Interoffice Memorandum

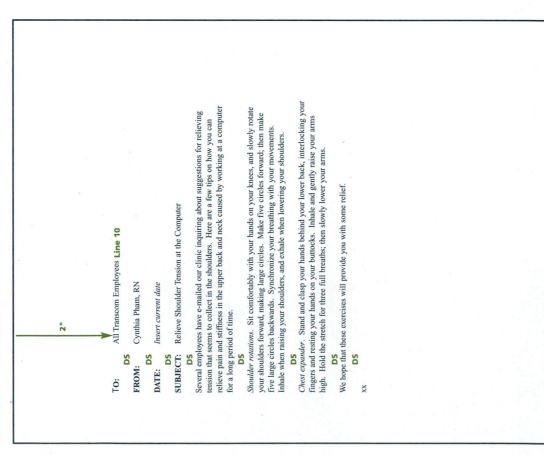

2"

TO: **DS**   All Transcom Employees **Line 10**

FROM: **DS**   Cynthia Pham, RN

DATE: **DS**   *Insert current date*

SUBJECT: **DS**   Relieve Shoulder Tension at the Computer

DS

Several employees have e-mailed our clinic inquiring about suggestions for relieving tension that seems to collect in the shoulders. Here are a few tips on how you can relieve pain and stiffness in the upper back and neck caused by working at a computer for a long period of time.

DS

Shoulder rotations. Sit comfortably with your hands on your knees, and slowly rotate your shoulders forward, making large circles. Make five circles forward; then make five large circles backwards. Synchronize your breathing with your movements. Inhale when raising your shoulders, and exhale when lowering your shoulders.

DS

Chest expander. Stand and clasp your hands behind your lower back, interlocking your fingers and resting your hands on your buttocks. Inhale and gently raise your arms high. Hold the stretch for three full breaths; then slowly lower your arms.

DS

We hope that these exercises will provide you with some relief.

DS

xx

Contingency Fee Agreement

CONTINGENCY FEE AGREEMENT

DS

XXX XXXXXXX vs. XXXX XXXXXXXXXXX

DS

I hereby retain the law offices of XXXXXX XXXXXXX as my lawyers in all cases of property damage or personal injury or any claim otherwise directly or indirectly therefrom.

DS

Should a recovery result by settlement before the filing of a complaint, attorney is to receive one-fourth (1/4) of this recovery; and I am to receive three-fourths (3/4), less any expenses or costs if these have been advanced by XXXXXX XXXXXXX.

Should a recovery, either by settlement, trial, or otherwise, not result, I am to owe attorney nothing for time and services.

It is agreed that if a settlement offer is tendered in the case by the defendants and XXXXXX XXXXXXX believes in good faith that settlement should be accepted and communicates this to client, and client does not agree to the settlement offer, XXXXXX XXXXXXX may require client to advance the reasonable costs of trial in the case. In the event that client refuses to accept a reasonable settlement offer and refuses to advance costs, client thereby agrees to permit XXXXXX XXXXXXX to withdraw from the case.

I hereby give XXXXXX XXXXXXX my power of attorney to execute all complaints, claims, contracts, settlements, checks, drafts, compromises, releases, dismissals, and orders as I could myself. I grant XXXXXX XXXXXXX as my attorney an assignment to the extent of his fees and expenses and costs advanced and a lien on my cause of action.

XXXXXX XXXXXXX is authorized to see and make copies of all my hospital and medical records of any kind.

DS
Date: _____

Client: _____

DS
We accept:
DS

Address _____

DS
(Telephone) _____

Business Address _____

(Business Telephone) _____

Bill of Sale

BILL OF SALE

QS

KNOW ALL MEN BY THESE PRESENTS that NATHAN J. GOODALL, 498 Syracuse Street, North West, Warren, Ohio 44483, herein referred to as Seller, in consideration of Four Hundred Fifty Dollars ($450.00), to Seller paid by MADELINE R. BARR, 173 Fowler Lane, Girard, Ohio 44420, herein referred to as Buyer. The receipt whereof is hereby acknowledged, does hereby grant, bargain, sell and convey to the said Buyer, her executors, administrators and assigns, the following described personal property, to wit: one (1) antique cedar chest, one (1) antique maple dining table with four (4) matching spindle chairs, and one (1) cherry, glass-front, four-shelf bookcase, to have and to hold the same onto the said Buyer, her executors, administrators and assigns forever.

DS

And the said Seller, for himself and for his heirs, executors and administrators, does hereby covenant with the said Buyer, her executors, administrators and assigns, that Seller is the true and lawful owner of the said described property hereby sold, and has full power to sell and convey the same; that the title, so conveyed, is clear, free, and unencumbered; and further that Seller will warrant and defend the same against all claims or demands of all persons whomsoever.

DS

IN WITNESS WHEREOF, the said Seller has hereunto set his hand and seal this 14th day of September, 20--.

TS

_____
TS
NATHAN J. GOODALL

STATE OF OHIO) ss.
COUNTY OF TRUMBULL)

← **2 spaces**

TS

Before me, a Notary Public in and for said State, personally appeared NATHAN J. GOODALL, who acknowledged that he did sign and seal the foregoing instrument and that the same is his free act and deed.

DS

IN TESTIMONY WHEREOF, I have hereunto set my official hand and seal, this 14th day of September, 20--.

TS

_____
DS
My commission expires:

Notice of Garnishment, page 1

AFFIDAVIT, ORDER AND NOTICE OF GARNISHMENT
(PERSONAL EARNINGS)
(O.R.C. 2716.02, .03, .04, .05, .06)

THE STATE OF OHIO
COUNTY OF XXXXXX.   ss

XXXXXXXXX Court
XXXXX, Ohio

XXXXX XXXXXXXX
xxxx Xxxxxx Xx.
Xxxxx, Xxxx xxxxx,
Plaintiff,

Docket No. XXXX   Page XXX
Case No. xx-xx-xxxx

vs.

XXXXXX XXXXXXX
xxxx Xxxxx Xxx,
Xxxxx, Xxxx xxxxx
Defendant.

AFFIDAVIT

The undersigned, being first duly cautioned and sworn, affirmed according to law, says that I am the XXXXX/attorney or agent for plaintiff herein, and that said plaintiff heretofore, to-wit, on the xxx day of Xxxx xx, duly recovered a judgment before this Court against said defendant XXXXXX XXXXXXXX.

AMOUNT NOW DUE $xxxx.xx

The affiant has good reason to believe and does believe that XXXXXX XXXXXXX is liable for money owing to said Judgment debtor for personal earnings, Section 2329.66, is subject to execution, attachment, or sale to satisfy a judgment or order under the laws of the state of Ohio.

And, that a true copy of the Demand, as required by Section 2716.02 of the Revised Code, was served upon the defendant herein by sending it by certified letter, return receipt requested, or by regular mail, evidenced by a properly completed and stamped certificate of mailing by regular mail, to his usual place of residence AND THAT DEFENDANT IS NOT IN THE MILITARY SERVICE OF THE UNITED STATES.

That the payment demanded in the notice required by Section 2716.02 of the Revised Code has not been made, nor has a sufficient portion been made to prevent the garnishment of personal earnings as described in Section 2716.02 of the Revised Code.

That affiant has no knowledge of any application by defendant for the appointment of a Trustee so as to preclude the garnishment of defendant's personal earnings.

That the affiant has no knowledge that the debt to which the affidavit pertains is the subject of a debt scheduling agreement of such a nature that it precludes the garnishment of the personal earnings of the defendant under division (B) of 2716.03.

ATTORNEY FOR PLAINTIFF
XXXX XXXXXX-XXXXXX
xx Xxxxx Xx., Xxxxx xxx
Xxxxx, Xxxx xxxxx

Sworn to and subscribed before me
this _____ day of _____, 20--

_____
NOTARY PUBLIC

Notice of Garnishment, page 2

SECTION A. COURT ORDER AND NOTICE OF GARNISHMENT

To: XXXXXX X. XXXXXXXXXX, Garnishee

The plaintiff in the above case has filed an affidavit, satisfactory to the undersigned, in the XXXXXX XXXXXX, XXXXXX XXXXXXXXXX Court stating that you owe the defendant money for personal earnings and that some of that money may not be exempt from execution or attachment under the laws of the State of Ohio.

Return the original of this form, together with any amount shown due thereon to the XXXXXX XXXXXX, XXXXXXX XXXXXXXXX Court not later than Xxxx xx, xxxx. Deliver one copy of this form and the enclosed documents entitled "Notice of Defendant" and "Request for Hearing" to the defendant. Keep the other copy of the form for your files.

The total amount of the

A. Plaintiff's Judgment is $x,xxx.xx
B. The Estimated Court Costs are $ xx.xx
C. The Total Probable Amount Owed is $x,xxx.xx

Witness my hand and the seal of this court this _____ day of _____, 20____.

_____
Judge

Complaint on Account

IN THE XXXXX MUNICIPAL COURT
XXXXXX COUNTY, XXXX
DS

XXXX X. XXXXXX
Xxxx Xxxxx Xxxxxx
Xxxxx, Xxxxx xxxxx

CASE NO.:

Plaintiff

JUDGE:

vs.

XXXXXXX X. XXXXXXX   COMPLAINT ON ACCOUNT
xxxx Xxxxxx Xxxxxx
Xxxxxxxx Xxxxx, Xxxx xxxxx
DS
Defendant
DS

Plaintiff, by and through xxx undersigned attorney, for cause of action against the defendant alleges:
DS

1. Defendant XXXXXXX X. XXXXXXX owes the plaintiff Xxx Xxxxxxxx Xxx Xxxxxxx Xxxxx-Xxx Dollars and Xxxxxx-Xxxxx Cents ($x,xxx.xx) according to the account hereto annexed as Exhibit "A."
DS
2. Said defendant has failed and refused to pay the balance due and owing although demand has been made.
3. Defendant also agreed to pay for plaintiff's reasonable attorney's fees in the event the account was placed for collection.
DS

WHEREFORE, plaintiff demands judgment against the defendant for the sum of Xxx Xxxxxxxx Xxx Xxxxxxx-Xxx and Xxxxxxx-Xxxxx Cents ($x,xxx.xx) and costs, plus interest at the rate of x% per annum from Xxxx x, xxxx, which includes the sum of Xxxx Xxxxxxxx Dollars ($xxx.xx) for reasonable attorney's fees.
DS

Respectfully submitted,
QS

XXXX XXXXXXX-XXXXXXX
Xxxxxxxx xxx xxx Xxxxxxxx
xxx Xxxxx Xxxxxx, Xxxxx xxx
Xxxxx, Xxxx xxxxx
(xxx) xxx-xxxx

Petition

IN THE COURT OF COMMON PLEAS
DOMESTIC RELATIONS DIVISION
FRANKLIN COUNTY, OHIO
DS

IN RE:
DS
THE DISSOLUTION OF
THE MARRIAGE OF: CASE NO.

DENNIS D. EWER   JUDGE ALTON C. CALL

and

PETITION FOR
SANDRA M. EWER,   DISSOLUTION OF MARRIAGE

Petitioners
TS

1. The parties have been residents of the State of Ohio for at least six (6) months immediately preceding the filing of this Petition and have been residents of Summit County for at least ninety (90) days immediately preceding the filing of this Petition.
DS
2. The parties were married on May 21, 1993, in Phoenix, Maricopa County, Arizona; no children have been born as issue of said marriage, and none are anticipated.
DS
3. The parties have agreed to and signed the attached Separation Agreement, and the same together with all amendments hereafter made is hereby incorporated into this Petition as if fully set forth herein.
DS

WHEREFORE, the parties petition the Court for a Decree of Dissolution of their marriage incorporating their Separation Agreement.
DS

Respectfully submitted,
DS

DENISE C. BLUM
Attorney for Petitioner,
Dennis D. Ewer
One Canal Plaza, Suite No. 800
Akron, Ohio 44307
(330) 555-0110
DS

DENNIS D. EWER, Petitioner
DS

SANDRA M. EWER, Petitioner

Mammogram Report

Radiology #: xxxx   DATE: x/xx/xx

DS

LOW DOSE MAMMOGRAM

DS

Xxx xxxxxxxxxx xx xxxxxxxx xxxx xxxxxxxx xxxxx xx xxxxxxxx, xxxxx xxxx xx xxxx xxx xxxxx xxxxx, xxxxxxxx xx xxx xxxxxxx xxxxxxxx xxx x xxxxx xx xxxxxxxx xxxxxxxxxxxxxxx xxxx xx xxxx xxxxx xxx xxxxxxx xxxxx. Xxxxx xxx xxxxxxxx xxx xxxxxxx xx xxxxxx. Xxx xxxxxxxx xxxxxxxxxxxxx xxxxx xxxx xxxxxxxxx xxxxxxx xxxx xx xxxxxxxxx xxxxxxxxx, xxx x xxxxxxx xx xxxxxxxxxxx xxxxx Xxxxx, xxxxxx xx xxx xxxxxxx x xxxxx. Xxxx xx xxxxxx xxxxxxxxx xxx xxxxxxxx, xxx x xxxxxx xx xxxxxxxxxx. Xxx xxxxxx, xxxxxx xx xxx xxxxxxxx xxxxxxx xxx x xxxxx xx xxxxxxxx xx xxxxxxx xx xxxxxxxxxx xx xxxxxx. Xxx xxxxxx xx xxxxxxxx x xxxxx. Xxxx xx xxxxxx xxxxxxxxx xxx xxxxxxxxxx, xxx x xxxxxxx xx xxxxxxxxxxx.

IMPRESSION:

1. Xxxxxxxxx xxxxxxx xxxxxxxx xxxxxxxxx xxxxxxxxx xx xxxxx xxxx xxxx xxxxxxx xxxxxxxxx xx xxx xxxxxx xxxxx xxx xxx xxx xxxxx xxxx xxxxx xxx xxxxxxx, xxx x xxxxx xxx xxxxxx xxxxxxxxxx.

2. Xx xxxxxxx, xxxxx xxx x xxx xxxxxxx xxxxxxxxxx xxxxxxxxx xx xxx xxxxx xxxxx xxxxxxx xxxxxxxx xxxxx xxx xxxxxxxxx xxxxx.

3. X xxx xxxxx xxxxxxx xxxxxxx xxxxxxx xxx xxxxxx xxxxxxxx xx xxx xxxxx xxxxx xxxxxx xxxx xx xxxxxxxxx xxxxxxxxxxxx.

Qs

Xxxxx Xxxx, X.X.
Xxxxxxxxxx

Qs

Xxxxxx X. Xxxxxx, X.X.   Xxxxxxxx, Xxxxxxx #xxxxx-x
D & T: x/xx/xx, x/xx/xx XX/xx
Dictated By: Xxxx Xxxx, X.X.

Report of Radiologist

Great Lakes Associates in Radiology and Imaging
777 St. Clair Avenue
Cleveland, OH 44114-3144
Phone: (216) 555-0111
Fax: (216) 555-0101

Patient's Name		Age	Address	X-Ray No.
Xxxxxx, Xxxxxx		(x/xx/xx) xx	xxxx Xxxxxxx Xxxx Xxxxx, XX xxxxx	xxx
Guarantor		Telephone		Date
xxxx		(xxx) xxx-xxxx		x/xx/xx
S.S. No.		Insurance Information		Referring Physician
xxx-xx-xxxx		XXXXXXXX		Xxxxxxx, X.
Previous Exam				Exam Requested
xx				xxxxxx xxxxx
History		Place of Employment		xx
xx		xx		

REPORT OF RADIOLOGIST

Xx. Xxxxxx Xxxxxxx, xxxx Xxxxxx Xxxx, Xxxxxxxx, XX xxxxx

DS

XXXXXX, XXXXXXX X.

DS

CLINICAL INDICATION: Xxxx xxxxxxxx xxx xxxx xxxx.

DS

LUMBAR SPINE: Xxxxx xx xxxxxxx xxxxxxxx xxx xxxxx xxxxx, xxxxx xx xxxxxxxxxxx xxxxxxxxx xxxxxxxx, xxxxx xx x xxxxx x xxxxxxxxxxx xxxxxxxx xx xx xxxxx xx, xx xxxxxxxxxxx xx xxxx; xxxxxxxxxx xxxxxxxx, xx xxxxxx xxxxxxxx xx xxxxx.

DS

IMPRESSION: Xxxxxxxx, xxxxx xx x xxxxx x xxxxxxxxxxxxx xx x xxxx xx. xx xxxxxxxxxxx xx; xxxx; xxxxxxxxx, xxxx xxxxxx xx xxx xx xxxxxxxxxx xxxxxxxxx xxxxx. xxxxxx xx; xxxxxxxx xxxxxxxxxx, xx xxxxxxxx xxxxxxxx xx xxxxxxxxxx xx xxxxx.

DS

PELVIS: Xxxxxxxx, xxxxx xx x xxxxx x xxxxxxxxxxxxx xxxx xx xxxxxxxxxx; xxxxxxxx, xxxx xxxxx xx xxx xx xxxxxxxxxx xxxxxxxx xx xxx xxxxxxx, xxxxx xx xxxxxxxx xxxxxxxxxx. xx xxxxxx xxxxxxx xx xxxxxxxxx xx xxxx.

DS

IMPRESSION: Xxxxxxxxxxxxxx xx xxx xxxxx xxx xxxxxx xxx xxxxxxxxxx xxxxxxxx xxxxxx xx xxxxxxxx.

Qs

Xxxxxx Xxxxxx, X.X. (xx)
2 spaces

Discharge Summary

DISCHARGE SUMMARY
DS

PATIENT NAME: Xxxxxx Xxxxxxx
DS
PATIENT NUMBER: xxx-xx-xxxx
DS
ADMISSION DATE: x/xx/xxxx
DS
DISCHARGE DATE: x/xx/xxxx
DS
ATTENDING PHYSICIAN: Xxxx Xxxxxx, X.X. X.X.X.X.
DS

Xxxxxx-xxxxx xxxx-xxx xxxxx xxxxxx xxx xxxxxxx xxxxxxxxx xx xxxxxxxxx xxxxx xxxxx xxxxx xxxx xxx x-xxxx xxxxxxx xx xxxxxxxxxxxxxxxx. Xx xxx xxxx xxxxxxxxx, xxxx xxxxxxxx xxx xxxxxxx xxxxxxxxxxx xxxx xxxxxxxx. Xxx xx xxxx xxx xxxxxxxx, xxx xxx xxx xxxxxxxxx xxxx xx xxx xxxxxxx xxxxxx-xx xxxx xx Xx. Xxxxxx.
DS

FINAL DIAGNOSIS: 1. Xxxxxxxxx xxxxxx, Xxxxxx xxxx.
    2. Xxx-xxxxxxxxxx xx xxx x xxxxxx.

2 spaces

QS

Signed _____
Xxxx Xxxxxx, X.X., X.X.X.X.
DS

xx

Operative Report

OPERATIVE REPORT
DS

NAME: Xxxxxx Xxxxxx   HOSPITAL NUMBER: xxx-xx-xxxx
DS
ADMISSION: Xxxxxxx xx, xxxx   ROOM: xxxxx
DS
DISCHARGE: Xxxxxxx xx, xxxx   DICTATED: Xxxxxxx xx, xxxx
DS
DATE OF PROCEDURE: Xxxxxxx xx, xxxx
DS
SURGEON: Xxxxxx Xxxxxxx, X.X.X.
DS
ASSISTANT: Xxxxxx Xxxxxx, X.X.X.
DS
PREOPERATIVE DIAGNOSIS: Xxxxxxxxxxxxx xxxxxxxxxxxx xxxxxxxxxxx xxxxxxxx.
DS
POSTOPERATIVE DIAGNOSIS: Xxxx.
DS
NAME OF OPERATION: Xxxxxxxxxx xxxxxxxx.
DS
ANESTHESIA: Xxxxxxxx xxxx xxxxxxxxxxx.
DS
DESCRIPTION OF PROCEDURE: Xxxx xxxxxxxxx xxx xxxxxxxx xxxxxxxxx xxx xx Xx. Xxxxx. Xxx xxxxxx xxxx xxx xxxxxxxx, xx xxxx xxxxxxx xxx xxxxxxxxxx, xxx x xxx xxxxxx xxxx xxxxxxxx xxxxxxxxxx xxx xxx xxxx xxxxx xxxxxxxxx xxxxx- xxx xxxxxxxxxx xxxxxx xxxx xxxxxxxxxxx xxx xxx xxxxxx xxxxxxxxx xxxx xxxxx xxxxxxxx. X Xxxxx xxxxxx xxxx xxxxxxx xxxxx xxx xxxx xx xxxxxx xxx xxxxxx xxx xxxx xxxxxxxxxxxxx. Xxxxxxxx xxxxxx xxxx xxxxx xxxxxx. Xxxxx xxx xx xxxxxx.
DS
COMPLICATIONS: Xxxx.
DS
ESTIMATED BLOOD LOSS: Xxxxxxx.
DS
REPLACEMENT: Xx xxxxxxxxx xxxxxxx.
DS
X-RAYS: Xxxx.
DS
SPECIMEN: Xxxx.

_____
Xxxxxx Xxxxxx, X.X.X.

xx

Here is a compilation of all the language skills rules arranged in alphabetical order for easy reference.

APOSTROPHE LANGUAGE SKILLS

1. Use an apostrophe to show contraction or the omission of figures.
   - hasn't for has not
   - '99 for 1999

2. Use an apostrophe to form the possessive of nouns:
   a. For a singular noun, add an apostrophe and **s**.
      - manager's office
   b. For a plural noun not ending in **s**, add an apostrophe and **s**.
      - women's issues
   c. For a plural noun ending in **s**, add only an apostrophe.
      - the players' uniforms

3. Use an apostrophe and s to form the plurals of figures, letters, symbols, and words.
   - Your 1's and 7's look alike, as do your t's and I's.

4. To form the possessive of a proper noun ending in an *s* or *z* sound (except *ce*):
   a. Add an apostrophe and *s* to words containing only one syllable.
      - Liz's software
   b. Add only an apostrophe to words of more than one syllable.
      - Dennis' policy

5. Form the possessive of a compound word by adding an apostrophe and *s* ('s) to its final syllable.
   - brother-in-law's apartment

6. Form the possessive of a series of names connected by a conjunction showing joint ownership by adding an apostrophe or an apostrophe and *s* ('s) to the final name in the series.
   - Hayes and Shultz's consulting firm

7. If joint ownership does not exist in a series of names, form the possessive by adding an apostrophe or an apostrophe and *s* ('s) to each proper name in the series.
   - Dan's, Gus's, and Larry's stations

8. Form the possessive of abbreviated words or acronyms by adding an apostrophe and *s* ('s) to the last letter.
   - YMCA's events
   - NATO's annual conference

CAPITALIZATION LANGUAGE SKILLS

1. Capitalize the first letter in a direct quotation.
   - Joni said, "You should start studying."

2. Capitalize the names of individuals, organizations, institutions, buildings, political parties, religious groups, nationalities, and races.
   - Bill Clinton, a Democrat from Arkansas, was President of the United States and lived in the White House.

3. Capitalize names of countries, cities, states, rivers, mountains, islands, oceans; sections of cities and streets; and commonly recognized names given to regions of countries.
   - Mount Waialeala is on Kauai in the Hawaiian Islands.

4. Capitalize the first letter of all important words in the titles of the main agencies of a government.
   - The Treasury Department controls the printing of United States paper currency.

5. Capitalize personal titles when they immediately precede individual names and are directly related to them. Do not capitalize titles following names, except in an address or signature line.
   - Marvin Cofer, dean of the College of Business, was the guest speaker.

6. Days of the week, months of the year, and holidays begin with capital letters. Capitalize seasons only when they are personified or are part of a specific title.
   - Thanksgiving Day is on Thursday, November 22, this year.
   - As Wicked Winter seems to stay with us forever, it is easy to get spring fever.

7. Capitalize compass directions, such as North and South, when they are used to name a particular part of the country or are part of a specific name. These words are not capitalized, however, when they merely indicate a general location or direction.
   - To view the best colors in the East, take I-91 north through Vermont.

8. Capitalize only the first word and important words in headings and titles. The word *the* is only capitalized when it is the first word of a title; prepositions and conjunctions are not capitalized unless they have four or more letters. **Note:** The title of a book may be underscored or keyed in all capital letters or typed in italics.
   * *Gone with the Wind* was a best seller.

COLON LANGUAGE SKILLS

1. Use the colon to introduce formally a word, list, statement, or question; a series of statements or questions; or a long quotation.
   * You need to equip your workstation with the following: a computer, a printer, a FAX machine, a telephone, and a transcriber.
   * The question is: How fast can you do it?

COMMA LANGUAGE SKILLS

1. Use a comma to set off a nonrestrictive phrase or subordinate clause. A nonrestrictive or subordinate clause cannot stand alone and is dependent upon the main clause.
   * My manager, who is British, is well respected.

2. Use a comma to separate coordinate clauses that are joined by the conjunctions *and, but, for, neither, nor,* and *or.* The comma is placed before the conjunction.
   * I left the office, but I forgot my briefcase.

3. Use a comma to set off phrases or expressions at the beginning of a sentence when they are loosely connected with the rest of the sentence.
   * However, you must submit your budget by Friday.

4. Use a comma to separate words, phrases, or clauses in a series. Use a comma before the last item in the series.
   * We lost our hard-copy files, our backup disk files, and the entire database in the fire.

5. Use a comma to set off parenthetical words, clauses, or phrases.
   * George, for example, has already completed his report.

6. Use a comma to separate unrelated numbers.
   - In 1993, 37 agencies reduced their costs.

7. Use a comma before a short, informal, direct quotation.
   - The assistant asked, "May I say who is calling?"

8. Use a comma to set off a dependent clause at the beginning of a sentence from the independent clause.
   - If the package doesn't come this morning, be sure to call me.

9. Use a comma or commas to set off a word or words that rename words they follow.
   - My best friend, Maria Sieradzki, moved away several weeks ago.

10. Use a comma to set off the name of a city from the name of the state and the name of the state from the rest of the sentence.
    - I live in Greenville, South Carolina, which is a beautiful city.

11. Use a comma or commas to set off adjectives of equal rank.
    - Her daughter was a beautiful, intelligent girl.

12. Use a comma to set off a prepositional phrase of four or more words at the beginning of a sentence. Do not use a comma to set off a prepositional phrase of less than four words.
    - In the first meeting, we elected officers.
    - In June we will get married.

13. Use a comma to set off the name of a person whom you are directly addressing.
    - Please open the door, Alice.

14. Use a comma to set off the date from the year and the year from the rest of the sentence.
    - We will receive the information on August 20, 2001, to make our final decision.

DASH LANGUAGE SKILLS

1. Use the dash to indicate a change in the sense or the construction of a sentence.
   - Robin, Walter, and Eve—these are people you can trust.

2. Use a dash instead of a comma for emphasis or to keep from confusing the reader.
   • If—and only if—the bill is paid, can we leave.

EXCLAMATION POINT LANGUAGE SKILLS

1. The exclamation point represents a full stop. It is used at the end of a thought expressing strong emotion or a command. This thought may be represented by a complete sentence, a phrase, or a word.
   • Wow! Look at that sunset!

HYPHEN LANGUAGE SKILLS

1. Use the hyphen to join compound numbers from twenty-one to ninety-nine when they are keyed as words.
   • forty-three
   • fifty-six

2. Use a hyphen to join compound adjectives before a noun they modify as a unit.
   • long-range plan
   • two-thirds majority

3. Use a hyphen after each word or figure in a series of words or figures that modify the same noun.
   • first-, second-, and third-class mail

4. Use a hyphen to show consecutive numbers or the passage of time, except when used with *from* or *between*.
   • People holding tickets numbered 0–499 will be admitted from 1:30–2:30 p.m.

NUMBER EXPRESSION LANGUAGE SKILLS

1. Amounts of money, except in legal documents, are written in figures. Amounts less than one dollar are written in figures with the word *cents* following. In writing even sums of money, omit the decimal and double zeros.
   • Our check for $49.49 was mailed today.
   • The customer was charged 50 cents for the gum.
   • Sue paid $11 for the book.

2. Except in formal or legal writing, the day of the month and the year are usually written in figures. When the date appears in the body of a letter, the year is customarily omitted if it is the same as that which appears on the dateline. It is not necessary to use *st*, *d*, or *th* in dates unless the day is written before or is separated from the month.
   - He will turn 50 on April 4, 1995; but we will celebrate on the 31st of March.

3. Spell out numbers ten and under unless they are used with other numbers that cannot be expressed conveniently in words or with numbers that exceed the number ten.
   - There are six days until the meeting.
   - We are sending 8 people from our home office of over 450 employees.

4. When two numbers immediately follow each other, spell out the smaller one and express the larger one in figures.
   - seven 100-pound bags

5. Use the abbreviations **a.m.** and **p.m.** with figures. Spell out the hour when *o'clock* is used.
   - Your flight is at 8:20 a.m. and will get you to Chicago in time for your three o'clock meeting.

6. Percentages are written in figures followed by a % sign in statistical data or the word *percent* in ordinary writing.
   - We need a 25 percent growth in membership.

7. Spell out numbers ten and below used for the names of streets; use figures for numbers above ten.
   - His office is on Sixth Avenue at 89th Street.

8. Spell out common fractions appearing alone in ordinary writing. Write mixed numbers as figures.
   - She sold one-half of the total crop.
   - I used 1 1/2 cups of sugar.

PARENTHESES LANGUAGE SKILLS

1. Use parentheses to enclose figures or letters that mark a series of enumerated elements within a paragraph.
    - The new business on the agenda will cover the following: (1) the building proposal, (2) the fund-raising program, and (3) the dues increase.

2. Use parentheses to enclose figures verifying a number that is spelled out.
    - fifty (50) dollars
    - fifty dollars ($50)

PERIOD LANGUAGE SKILLS

1. Use a period after a complete declarative or imperative sentence or a courtesy question.
    - The meeting will begin. Will you please take your seats.

2. Use a period after initials in a name.
    - E. J. Shultz

QUESTION MARK LANGUAGE SKILLS

1. Use a question mark after a direct question. Use a period after an indirect question or polite request.
    - What was his answer to our proposal?
    - She asked what letter I wanted.
    - Would you please shut the door.

2. Use a question mark after each question in a series if special emphasis is desired. When it is used this way, it takes the place of a comma and each element begins with a lowercase letter.
    - Are you prepared for layoffs? budget cuts? reduced benefits?

QUOTATION MARKS LANGUAGE SKILLS

1. Use quotation marks to enclose direct quotations. Use single quotation marks to enclose a quotation within a quotation. Always place the period or comma inside the quotation marks.
   - Jessica said, "He is one of the most 'hard-nosed' bosses I have ever known."

2. Use quotation marks to enclose unusual or slang terms, words used in some special sense, or words to which attention is directed in order to make a meaning clear.
   - Some people go "ballistic" if they hear someone misuse the words "lie" and "lay."

3. Use quotation marks to enclose the titles of articles, songs, poems, lectures, radio programs, television shows, and so on. Also, use quotation marks to enclose the titles of subdivisions of publications, such as parts or chapters. The titles of books and magazines are not enclosed in quotation marks but are underscored or keyed in all capital letters or italicized.
   - I enjoyed the chapter "Understanding Grammar" in the book PRACTICAL BUSINESS ENGLISH.
   - She sang "America the Beautiful" with real feeling.

SEMICOLON LANGUAGE SKILLS

1. In a compound sentence, use a semicolon between clauses that are not joined by a conjunction.
   - The report was well written; it was on time, too.

2. Use a semicolon in a compound sentence if either clause contains one or more commas. The semicolon is placed before the conjunction.
   - The hot, humid day made him irritable; but he would not turn on the air conditioning, turn on a fan, or open a window.

3. Use a semicolon before such words and abbreviations as *for example*, *namely*, *e.g.*, *i.e.*, *viz.*, and *to wit* when they introduce a long list of items. (A comma precedes the list.)
   - We need to buy office supplies; for example, envelopes, disks, copy paper, and toner cartridges.

4. Use a semicolon between elements in a listing when there are commas within the elements.
   - Our trip will take us to Washington, D.C.; New York, New York; Boston, Massachusetts; and Bangor, Maine.

5. Use a semicolon before connectives when such words introduce sentences, principal clauses, or abrupt changes in thought. A comma follows the connective when it is used in this manner only if the connective is to be emphasized. Some of these connectives are *accordingly, consequently, hence, however, in fact, moreover, nevertheless, therefore, thus, whereas, yet.*
   - His flight was canceled; therefore, we will delay the meeting.

WORD DIVISION LANGUAGE SKILLS

1. Leave enough of the word on the upper line to suggest the meaning of the entire word.
   - arrange-ment *not* ar-rangement

2. When dividing a word, the first part of the word must contain at least two letters and the last part of the word must contain at least three letters.
   - an-other *not* anoth-er

3. Avoid awkward or misleading divisions that may cause difficulty when reading.
   - carry-ing *not* car-rying

4. When a word containing three or more syllables is to be divided at a one-letter syllable, key the one-letter syllable on the upper line rather than on the lower.
   - maga-zine *not* mag-azine

5. When a word is divided at a point where two vowels that are pronounced separately come together, divide these vowels into separate syllables.
   - situ-ation *not* sit-uation *or* situa-tion

6. Divide compound words and hyphenated words between the elements of the compound and/or at the hyphen.
   - check-book *for* checkbook
   - self- made *for* self-made

7. Avoid the division of figures ($1,699.23) in the parts of an address or in a date. If it is necessary to separate an address, keep together the number and street name, the city, state, and ZIP Code. If it is necessary to divide a date, do so between the day and the year.

   • The company that we purchased is located at 1231 Dixon Avenue, Nashville, TN 37203–6109.

   • The conference will be held in Ohio on Tuesday, August 31, 2001.

8. When a suffix is added to a word that ends in double letters, divide the word after the double letters. If a final consonant is doubled when a suffix is added to a word, divide the word between the double letters.

   • fill-ing

   • refer-ring

9. If there are double consonants in a base word, divide the word between the double consonants.

   • recom-mend

10. Avoid dividing words at the end of two successive lines.

11. If using word processing software, hyphenation features may already be installed. Also, widow/orphan protection may be in place. Refer to your software reference manual.

Part 1—Basic Machine Transcription / Part 2—Intermediate Machine Transcription

	1	2	3	4	5	6	7	8	9	10	11	12
	Chapters						Chapters					
Composition Reinforcement												
Collaborative Research												
Transcription Exercises												
Proofreading Exercise												
Written Test												
Transcription Test												

Part 3—Advanced Machine Transcription / Part 4—Dictation and Continuous Speech Recognition

	13	14	15	16	17	18	19	20	
	Chapters								Part 4—Dictation and Continuous Speech Recognition
Composition Reinforcement									
Collaborative Research									
Transcription Exercises (Dictation/Transcription Exercises for Part 4)									
Proofreading Exercise									
Written Test									
Transcription Test									